exploring a great spiritual practice

journalkeeping

■ ■ ■ ■ ■ ■ ■ ■ ■ ■

Carl J. Koch
John Kirvan, series editor

 SORIN BOOKS™ Notre Dame, Indiana

www.avemariapress.com

International Standard Book Number: 1-893732-67-3

Cover and text design by Katherine Robinson Coleman

Photography: AP wide World Photos p. 21

Printed and bound in the United States of America.

Library of Congress Cataloging-in-Publication Data

Koch, Carl, 1945-
  Journal keeping / Carl J. Koch.
      p. cm. — (Exploring a great spiritual practice)
  Includes bibliographical references (p.   ).
  ISBN 1-893732-67-3 (pbk.)
  1. Spiritual journals—Authorship. 2. Diaries—Authorship—Religious aspects.
  I. Title. II. Series.
  BL628.5 .K63 2003
  248.4'6—dc22

                                                    2003021452

journalkeeping

Contents

chapterone

The**Journal Phenomenon**

"I feel happy to be keeping a journal again. I've missed it, missed naming things as they appear, missed the half hour when I push all duties aside and savor the experience of being alive in this beautiful place."

May Sarton

Whether you are already keeping a diary or just thinking about starting a journal, you can be sure of three things:

- ❧ You are not alone.

- ❧ Your age is not an issue.

- ❧ What you are doing is carrying on a tradition that is almost as old as humanity itself.

There are millions whose journal keeping has begun with a small lined-page book with a cover that reads "Dear Diary" or "My Secret Diary" and a tiny padlock that keeps the volume securely fastened. Every year millions of these disappear off bookstore shelves as gifts for young people wishing to pour out their private thoughts and secret feelings. For many of them, these Dear Diaries begin a practice that they will carry on well into their adulthood, the diary being the one place where they can say what they want and not be laughed at or thought foolish.

This year an estimated ten million blank journals will be sold to adults in U.S. bookstores and gift shops. And given that many of us keep our journals in spiral notebooks bought just about anywhere and still others of us keep our diaries on computers, the number of journal writers is huge.

Type "journal writing" into any Web search engine and hundreds of Web sites will appear on your screen. One online bookstore listed 15,345 titles when "diary" was entered as the search word.

What's more there is a journal for everyone.

JournalDepot.com sells twenty-six different types of journals. A journal writer can buy: art theme journals, baby journals, collector's journals, dream journals, fitness and health journals, home and cooking journals, parenting journals, relationship journals, religious journals, solid color journals, wedding journals, wine journals, women's journals. The most intriguing to me was the "other journal" that was probably for people who could not make up their minds, about which of the other twenty-five to buy. Then, under each category of journal, a buyer can select from among a dozen or so special journals.

At higherawareness.com a newcomer to the art of journaling can take an online course and learn about the benefits of using various journal tools, how to use the workbook, and setting up a journal. WritingtheJourney.com also offers workshops, features, famous journals, and even a survey. Many universities instruct their students about how to begin journal writing as part of composition or creative writing classes. The instructions online sometimes allow for interactive journal exchange with a journal ring and with the professor. Other Web sites give helpful advice to elementary teachers about how to use journal writing to enhance the language skills and self-expression of their young students. Many Web sites about journal keeping, like journaltherapy.com, provide information and instructions for the therapeutic uses of the journal.

And of course, www.intensivejournal.org explains the mission, summarizes the biography, and gives quotes from perhaps the most important figure in modern journal writing, Dr. Ira Progoff. Student of C. G. Jung, psychotherapist, and researcher, Progoff "found that the clients who wrote in some form of journal were able to work through issues more rapidly." In the 1960s and 1970s he developed his Intensive Journal Method and began conducting the Intensive Journal Workshop all over North America. His book *At a Journal Workshop* (1966) sold widely and became the bible of journal writers. More than 175,000 people are reported to have participated in the Intensive Journal Workshops.

Many memoirs, one of today's most popular and significant literary forms, are actually journals or adaptations of journals. *Angela's Ashes* by Frank McCourt and *The Liar's Club: A Memoir* by Mary Karr are two obvious examples of memoir bestsellers. The diaries of Anaïs Nin begun in the 1930s remain in print and continue to intrigue readers. And every year new personal stories capture the fascination of large audiences.

Clearly, published journals and memoirs, books, and Web sites about diary and memoir writing influence millions of people. But there is nothing new about journal keeping. The desire to tell our story is as old as human communication and remains an inherent passion for most human beings.

Personal stories transmit a set of personal and communal experiences and the values attached to those experiences. This partly explains what has always motivated people to tell their stories: They want people now and in future generations to know who they were, what happened, and what they stood for.

Memoir begins long before written language. In southern France, early humans painted pictures in caves to memorialize their hunting prowess. Pictured there are representations of the animals they killed and other figures one can presume were important to them. It's easy to imagine a clan of these cave-dwellers coming home from

> "The Intensive Journal process is our inner workshop, the place where we do the creative shaping of the artwork of our life."
>
> *Ira Progoff*

the hunt, triumphant and happy, then gathering around a fire. A storyteller launches into a recounting of the day's deeds: who threw the first spear, who darted under the tusks so bravely, and so on. Then, some days later, the clan's artist paints figures on the cave walls in an attempt to record the events so important to the clan's survival. Early memoir.

Go forward many centuries. Out in the arid lands of what is now Palestine, a tribe of nomads listens as the elders tell of their ancestor Abraham, who was chosen by God to create a great people. Then they tell of Isaac's deeds and how God led the people. As these stories grew in the consciousness of the people, many other stories and proverbs, songs and lamentations were added to become

one great story. As writing developed, teachers and scribes began writing the stories down for posterity. These memoirs became the Bible.

In Egypt, pharaohs were filling their tombs with pictures and hieroglyphics that told of their mighty deeds. In China, an early emperor reigning in Xian filled his tomb with artifacts, memorial tablets, a whole army of terracotta soldiers to protect him, and the corpses of the workers who built the tomb—all in an attempt to keep his story alive in the afterlife. These were memoirs on the grand scale.

As writing developed, generation after generation of people have written diaries, journals, or memoirs, whether on papyrus scrolls, vellum or animal skins, clay tablets, lined notebooks, blank sheets of paper in a typewriter, or in the secret files in their computers. Many ancient diaries remain. In chapter 2, references are made to the journals of the Roman Emperor Marcus Aurelius living in the second century C.E., whose daily reflections have come to us as *Meditations,* and to Egeria, a noble woman living in the fifth century, whose diary from her pilgrimage to the Holy Land is still read today.

In England, ten centuries after Egeria, Margery Kempe was recording her adventures in a diary. A wife and a mother of fourteen children, Margery still managed to go on pilgrimages to Jerusalem and Rome. All along the way, she wrote her observations and reflections. In chapter 18 of her journal, she describes an encounter with another keeper of a journal, the saintly anchoress Julian of Norwich, who was well known as a spiritual advisor. After Margery told Julian of God's graces in her life, Margery records Julian's response:

The anchoress, hearing the marvelous goodness of Our Lord, highly thanked God with all her heart for His visitation, counseling this creature to be obedient to the will of Our Lord God and to fulfill with all her might whatever He put into her soul, if it were not against the worship of God, and profit of her fellow Christians.

Margery found in Julian a kindred spirit. For her part, Julian had already recorded her own sacred revelations in her journal, later called *Showings*. Indeed, when scholars were collecting writing in English for an anthology of literature by women, they found that the first important writing in English was none other than Julian's *Showings*.

In the 1660s, Samuel Pepys diligently wrote his famous journal. In the next century, Benjamin Franklin, George Washington, Sarah Cordelia Wright, Sir Joseph Banks, and Thomas Jefferson took out their goose quills, sharpened and inked them, and wrote their thoughts. In the last century, as diverse a group as Bobby Sands, the Irish hunger striker, Theodore Roosevelt, and Elvis Presley all left diaries.

Clearly, there would be many more diaries in existence if more of the world's people had been literate. Well into the twentieth century, more than half of the globe's human population could not read, much less write. Even if people could write, paper and writing instruments came with a steep price. Few people except nobility and clergy, merchants and monks could afford the wherewithal to write anything. Nevertheless, their stories were told, but in songs and tales remembered and repeated by bards and troubadours.

The journal-memoir fills a basic need in human beings. Diarists and memoirists feel compelled to tell their stories, open their hearts to distant friends, or simply keep records of their daily lives. In the journal they honor their life, see its shape, struggle sometimes to reshape it, and offer us a glimpse of their wisdom and wit.

A sure sign that journal-memoir writing is robust in our times is the amount of newsprint dedicated to them. Not so long ago, *The New York Times Magazine* devoted an entire edition to "The Age of the Literary Memoir." James Atlas introduced the edition by saying, "It began, like any revolution, almost imperceptibly. . . . But if the moment of inception is hard to locate, the triumph of memoir is now established fact." Atlas tries to describe the reasons for the incredible interest in personal stories by quoting Mary Karr, author of the best-selling memoir *The Liar's Club*: "People want a window on how to behave." Offering stories as models of behavior has always been the function of personal narratives.

During the same year, *The Los Angeles Times* published a feature article by John Balzar that attempts to understand the phenomenon. Balzar quotes memoirist Tristine Rainer who says, "We have reached a point where, like primitive

> "I want to record **how the world comes at me,** because I think it is indicative of **the way it comes at everyone.**"
>
> *Philip Lopate*

people of old, the meaning of life comes with the stories we tell about it." Naomi Mann, another journal-memoir writer, offered him this explanation for why she collected her writing into a manuscript: "It's a way to unscramble chaos, to which all good art strives. . . . Today, there are no authority figures to transmit the legends and myths and experiences that help us understand ourselves." Again, the journal functions as a means of personal and communal grounding. It provides a base for growth.

One person who knows this intimately is Jim Cummings of Knapp, Wisconsin, who may have collected the most extensive private library of diaries in the world. When Peg Meier's article appeared in the *Minneapolis Star-Tribune*, Cummings owned more than sixteen thousand published diaries. But Cummings is not just a collector of other people's memoirs; each day Cummings writes in his own diary and has been doing so for forty-eight years, having begun at age thirteen. Why does he both keep a diary and collect those of other people?

He told Meier: "The diaries keep me from doing some things I'm not proud of. I can't do something awful and record it five hours later. My children and grandchildren may read the diaries someday. . . . I try to learn from myself. I write what I do, what I think, what I feel." Meier adds, "Diary-keeping makes him want to *lead* an interesting life, . . . so that he can *record* an interesting life."

"To me," Cummings has said, "a diary is a record of verification. It is a proof that one has lived and that one has cared enough about a precious life to describe it—Life whizzes by so fast, but I find I can brake it a bit by keeping a diary."

Cummings is right. Writing a diary is proof that one has lived, but it is so much more. And that "more" is the subject of the rest of this book.

chapter**two**

WritingforOur
Spirit'sSake

"For a spiritual quest means precisely . . . not starting in a vacuum at square one, but starting where we are with what we have and with what we have found, to quest for it again."

Jaroslav Pelikan

Keeping a Journal, A Perennial Practice

On campaign against the German tribes, the Roman Emperor Marcus Aurelius (121–180 c. e.) repaired to his tent each night. There he would sit at his camp table and write his meditations on the day, his thoughts addressed to himself. Marcus Aurelius did not write his *Meditations* for publication but rather to think through how he was conducting his life. He reflects, "Remember to retire into this little territory of your own, and above all do not distract or strain yourself. Be free, and look at things as a human, as a citizen, as a mortal. . . . Look within. Within is the fountain of good, and it will always bubble up, if you will ever dig." The *Meditations* of Marcus Aurelius are still being read among the great books of wisdom of western civilization.

Three centuries later, an educated, high-ranking woman, Egeria, ended her evenings by writing about the religious sites and holy women and men that she had met that day. Her journal, *Egeria: Diary of a Pilgrimage,* not only provides invaluable insights into the holy places and people of those early centuries of Christianity, but also into her spirit—her courage and fears, faith and wonder. After climbing Mount Sinai, she writes: "Surely here is something very wonderful, and without God's grace I do not think that it would be possible." After visiting sacred places in Egypt, the Sinai, and Jerusalem, Egeria says, "In the name of God, I decided to return to my homeland, for three full years had now elapsed since my coming to Jerusalem, and I had seen all the holy places to which I had been drawn to pray. Nevertheless, by the will of God, I wished to go to Mesopotamia of Syria, to visit the holy monks who were said to be numerous there." Part travelogue and part personal reflections, Egeria's diary gave her a space to ponder her spirituality and later remember her pilgrimage.

The urge to write about personal experiences and the state of one's spirit stretches well into our own time. On June 20, 1942, while hiding from the Nazis, thirteen-year-old Anne Frank kept her touching, brave diary: "I can never bring myself to talk of anything outside the common round. . . . Perhaps I lack confidence, but anyway, there it is, a stubborn fact and I don't seem to be able to do anything about it. Hence, this diary. . . I want this diary itself to be my friend, and I shall call my friend Kitty."

Fifty years later, June 29, 1992, an 11-year-old girl, Zlata Filipovic, living among the carnage and chaos of Sarajevo, addresses her diary:

Dear Mimmy,

BOREDOM!!! SHOOTING!!! SHELLING!!! PEOPLE BEING KILLED!!! DESPAIR!!! HUNGER!!! MISERY!!! FEAR!!!

That's my life! . . . In short, a childhood without a childhood. . . . God, will this ever stop, will I ever be a schoolgirl again, will I ever enjoy my childhood again? . . .

Your Zlata

Journal or diary writing is a perennial practice because it is such a helpful way of honoring, pondering, and learning from life's journey. Saying that life is a journey or a pilgrimage has become a cliché; it's also true. To gain full appreciation and understanding of the journey requires that a person be conscious of what's happening. Flying into Grand Canyon is exciting and magnificent, only if I have a willing spirit and open eyes. Then to gain wisdom along the way demands that I reflect on what happens. Thus, the journal.

When I was a school administrator conducting a search for new faculty, I would receive letters of recommendation. One phrase that often showed up on the letters was some variation of "Ms. X has eight years experience teaching algebra." This could mean that Ms. X had grown to be a fine teacher because each year of the eight she had learned to be more effective. The phrase could also mean that Ms. X taught the same year over and over eight times. In other words, going on a pilgrimage—living eight, sixteen, thirty-two years—can be filled with growth if we reflect on and learn from it or it can be the same year lived over and over.

As the practice of as diverse a group as Marcus Aurelius, Egeria, Anne Frank, and Zlata shows, one way of keeping track of and learning from our years is by writing about them, day by day. A time-tested way of staying in tune with experiences, remembering lessons learned, recollecting important moments and people is keeping a diary, a journal, or a log.

We Are Our Story

Every entry in our journal is a story of our life as it unfolds. If I describe a chance encounter with an old friend, I am recapturing a part of who I am and where I have been. If I write furiously about anger boiling over an injustice done at work, I am unveiling a side to myself that

"Gaining access to that interior life is a kind of . . . archaeology: on the basis of some information and a little bit of guesswork you journey to a site to see what remains were left behind and you reconstruct the world."

Toni Morrison

could, if hidden, fester into bitterness or depression. We are our story, and it's best told, even if only for our own hearing.

Frederick Buechner, minister and novelist, remarked once, "My story is important not because it is mine . . . but because if I tell it anything like right, the chances are you will recognize that in many ways it is yours. Maybe nothing is more important than that we keep track . . . of these stories of who we are and where we have come from and the people we have met along the way because it is precisely through these stories in all their particularity . . . that God makes himself known to each of us most powerfully and personally. . . . To lose track of our stories is to be profoundly impoverished not only humanly but spiritually." In the story, writers meet themselves and meet their God.

Writing gives the writer's story tangible form, makes it objective so that she or he can look at it later and see what lessons it has to offer. And every lesson is a blessing. In *Remembered Rapture,* Bell Hooks describes this kind of inner archaeology:

> Living a life in the spirit, living faith, means that I must be ever vigilant, critically interrogating my actions, my words. Martin Luther King, Jr. encouraged spiritual vigilance, confessing that "I subject myself to self-purification and to endless self-analysis; I question and soul-search constantly into myself to be as certain as I can that I am fulfilling the true meaning of my work. . . ." Often before I write or speak, I pray, asking in the words that I learned as a child that 'the words of my mouth and the meditation of my heart be acceptable in thy sight.' These moments of prayer remind me of my spiritual task. It is my hope and my experience that they temper the ego and deepen my compassion.

> "Everything that happens is either a **blessing** which is also a lesson, or a lesson which is also a **blessing.**"
>
> *Polly Berrien Berends*

For many journal writers, unwrapping and telling their stories lifts before their consciousness aspects of their story that help them realize that they are not alone in the universe: Their story is everyone's story. And from that discovery can flow compassion, day by day.

In fact, the word "journal" has its roots in the French word "jour," meaning day. A journal is a record of a day's journey, the distance covered in a day's travel. "Diary" comes from the Latin word "dies," meaning day. In keeping a journal or diary, writers honor the unfolding story of their lives. In witnessing the day, they are paying attention to how they live. From this can come wisdom and enlightenment.

Write!

This journal experience is helpful for diarists wishing to review their inner landscape:

1. Quickly, spontaneously list as many religious or spiritual events as you can: These are moments on your spiritual journey during which you experienced the presence of the Holy, your Higher Power, Ultimate Value, God. Get down on paper as many instances as you can.

2. Next, pick one moment that you remember vividly and narrate it. Like narrating any story, tell how it began, describe the middle and the ending.

3. Finally, in writing, ponder how this story has influenced the shape of your life.

Our Story—The Shape of Our Spirituality

Our story tells us what our spirituality is all about, and our spirituality helps shape our story. To understand this, it is necessary to describe what "spirituality" is. Here are some useful descriptions by different writers on spirituality:

"How do I know what **I think** until I see what I say?"

E. M. Forster

Spirituality is the style of a person's response to God before the challenge of everyday life in a given historical and cultural environment. (Katherine Dyckman and Patrick Carroll)

Spirituality is . . . theology walking. (Joan Chittister)

Spirituality is the whole of one's spiritual or religious experience, one's beliefs, convictions, and patterns of thought, one's emotions and behavior in respect to what is ultimate, or to God. (Ann Carr)

The elements of these descriptions can be summed up this way:

Spirituality is the lived experience of our beliefs.

Beliefs shape the way we act. If we believe that we should behave honestly and with kindness, we tend to tell the truth, respond politely, give to charity, and so on.

Our lived experience shapes our beliefs. If, on balance, people treat us honestly and with kindness, we grow in the belief that most people are trustworthy and kind.

Our lived experience and our beliefs are always interacting, always informing one another and forming our spirituality.

If we are our story, our spirituality is our story. Story tells us what our spirituality is, and our spirituality shapes our story: the lived experience of our beliefs. This relationship between story and spirituality can be understood by recalling how the Bible came about. After all, the Bible is the story—the lived experience—of a people's belief in the God of Abraham. From Genesis to Revelation, the Bible is filled with the stories of people's experiences or encounters with the Holy One.

"To awaken, **to open up like a flower** to the light of a fuller consciousness! I want to **see and feel and expand,** little book, you holder of my secrets."

Emily Carr

In like manner, the spirituality of Buddhism has developed as followers tried to live the teachings of Siddartha Gautama. Buddhists remembered his words, recorded them, and passed them on to others. New stories were added that reflected evolving wisdom from the lived experience of those original teachings. Spirituality and story are living things; they grow and develop in the interplay of experience and belief.

"Those who know others are **wise**. Those who know themselves are **enlightened**."

Lao-Tzu

Soul Growing

There's a lot of talk about spiritual growth in popular, self-help magazines. Many serious books offer ancient wisdom about soul-growing. What is commonly found in the literature of spiritual growth is this:

We know that we are growing spiritually when each choice we make nurtures and aligns with our beliefs, and our love becomes more and more inclusive.

As our decisions consistently reflect our beliefs, we act with internal harmony. When my beliefs and actions coincide, then I am growing spiritually. People best understand this when their actions contradict what they really believe. For instance, when I fly into a rage, instead of stopping to reflect before I act or when I make snide remarks about someone instead of listening better and keeping my mouth shut, I feel all wrong. In other words, when conscience kicks in and reminds me that I am not acting as I believe I should, I know that my spirituality needs realignment.

The second criteria—our love becomes more and more inclusive—has its roots in all the world's great religious traditions. Love—fostering the best good of others, compassion, kindness, or charity form the core moral principle by which all actions can be said to be good or evil. Buddhism teaches compassion for all living things. The fasting of Ramadan reminds devout Muslims that they should have empathy for and give alms to poor people whose hunger is a daily misery. Judaism and Christianity declare that their followers should love God and love their neighbors as themselves. In short, the ability to love more inclusively stands as a key criteria of spiritual growth.

So how does writing a diary or journal help a person grow in spirit? Honest, spontaneous, reflective writing becomes meditation on

(1) how our actions align with our beliefs and (2) how we are learning to love.

Meditation means to pay attention, to offer awareness, to take "a long, loving look at the real" as one ancient writer said. By taking the time to sit and describe the day's unfolding, remember in writing some important moment on the journey, record the blessings of the day, or copy an inspiring quote, diarists are bringing their awareness to their experience, to their story. They throw the light of attention on their lived experience to see if it reflects their beliefs. By the same token, pondering their lived experience may tell them that some of their beliefs are too narrow, erroneous, or destructive.

In the diary, journal writers ask themselves and answer on paper soul-growing questions like: What is my life like? What did I do today that was a blessing? How do I feel about my relationship with X? And so on. Writing in this way leads them on the path of self-knowledge that Teresa of Avila talked about when she said: "This path of self knowledge must never be abandoned, nor is there on this journey a soul so much a giant that it has no need to return often to the stage of an infant and a suckling. And this should never be forgotten." Self-knowledge and spiritual growth walk the same path hand-in-hand.

Human beings change themselves and grow spiritually by changing the small assertions of self, namely their acts.

This wise adage provides a helpful way of thinking about the way people grow spiritually:

Plant an act; reap a habit.

Plant a habit; reap a virtue or vice.

Plant a virtue or vice; reap a character.

Plant a character; reap a destiny.

Developing character and destiny—growing to spiritual fullness—begins with the acts that each person plants each day, whether consciously or unconsciously. Each person's character is the combination of his or her virtues and vices. Their destiny is what finally becomes of them. The whole process begins in individual actions, but all the pieces interact.

In his memoir, *Returning: A Spiritual Journey*, Dan Wakefield recounts how he became aware of the integration of actions, spirit, character, and keeping a journal of the story of his life:

> For most of my life I kept a journal to record thoughts, impressions, conversations, scenes, and events, and after I started going to church I got another notebook to keep as a kind of "spiritual journal" for all that was happening to me in the new and growing awareness of that realm. I kept those segregated journals for several years . . . until one day. . . I started laughing at the

naivete of my notion that it was possible to compartmentalize the spiritual or religious side of one's experience like a separate subject or course in school, and I combined the pages of the two notebooks into one.

"You need only claim the events of your life to make yourself yours. When you truly possess all you have been and done, which make take some time, you are fierce with reality."

Florida Scott-Maxwell

The past and present, actions and beliefs compose one story; they are not separate. Wakefield's destiny is rooted in his actions, but these actions constantly interact with beliefs, experiences, and relationships—the rest of his life.

The journal is a time-tested way to look carefully at our actions—past, present, and future—and the ways these actions grow into habits, virtues or vices, and character, so that we create destinies filled with brilliant light and rich love.

Write!

Many writers find that simply posing key questions to themselves on paper and then writing reflections deepens their awareness. A simple exercise for understanding the place of love in a person's life starts with having some blank sheets of paper and a favorite pen in hand.

1. Take a few deep breaths and then ask yourself this question: How do I love?

2. Then, just start writing whatever responses come to mind and heart. If you get distracted and start going off somewhere else, gently come back to the question, "How do I love?" and keep writing.

Some diarists keep writing their responses for a week, every month, regularly each year. "How do I love?" is a central question for spiritual growth, one that should stay before anyone seeking fuller living.

> "What **spiritual growth** does is expand the range and **depth of my love** and my capacity for relationships. It enables me to retain **my integrity** while incorporating greater contrasts into my life."
>
> *Kathleen Fischer*

Other Spiritual Benefits of Writing a Journal

Writing a journal or diary can be healing. Healing means becoming whole or complete. When we cut ourselves, we know that we have healed when the two flaps of skin knit together again and become one solid stretch of flesh. Spiritual healing happens when we live in harmony with our beliefs. The diary or journal helps us keep track of our lives and put the pieces together when we become frazzled and overwhelmed. In her famous diaries, Anaïs Nin declared, "The false person I had created for the enjoyment of my friends, the gaiety, the buoyant, the receptive, the healing person, always on call, always ready with sympathy, had to have its existence somewhere. In the diary I could reestablish the balance. Here I could be depressed, angry, disparaging, discouraged. I could let out my demons." In writing the reality of her life, Nin saw herself whole.

Journal writing can be a great release. This letting out of feelings on paper instead of in violent words, scenes of agony, or acts of envious rage gives us a way to calm the inner dragons. Poet Sylvia Plath, a woman filled with torment, confessed, "Fury jams the gullet and spreads poison, but, as soon as I start to write, dissipates, flows out into the figure of the letters."

Journal writing can be freeing. Ray Bradbury is best known for his science fiction. Many of the insights that make his novels and stories so intriguing came from the kind of reflection that emerged from his other, more personal writing. Bradbury once concluded: "In a lifetime, we stuff ourselves with sounds, sights, smells, tastes, and textures of people, animals, landscapes, events, large and small. We stuff ourselves with these impressions and experiences and our reactions to them. Into our subconscious go not only factual data but reactive data, our movement toward or away from the sensed event. . . . This is the storehouse, the file, to which we must return every waking hour to check reality against memory." All human beings are susceptible to the constant bombardment of impressions that flood the subconscious, and the sad truth is most of them are false. Nevertheless, without conscious reflection they can enslave us.

Freedom is our capacity to take part in shaping our life. To shape our life, we first have to be conscious. Conscious living comes through the process of writing. As we write out our feelings, dreams, hopes, fears, encounters, worries, and joys, we more fully understand the wholeness of who we are. Without this consciousness automatic impulses, knee-jerk reactions, prejudices, and ignorance more easily push us along. Psychologist Carl Jung concluded, "When we are unconscious of a thing . . . it moves us or activates us as if we were marionettes. We can only escape that effect by making it conscious and objectifying it, putting it outside ourselves, taking it out of the unconscious." When we write things down, no matter how painful or pleasant, shameful or glorious, the experiences take objective form on the page that we can ponder and understand. Then we can discern more freely how to act.

Journal writing honors our encounters with the Spirit. By writing about our days, we increase our awareness of the Spirit's touch through people, in nature, and in ourselves. According to the Christian Testament, within each person is "the Spirit of truth" an "Advocate" (see John 14). In the Hindu scriptures, the spirit inside each person is named *Atman*, which is indistinguishable from *Brahman*, the divine spirit. While writing about our encounters with the Spirit, we can consciously begin to move in step with the will of the Divine toward compassion, love, and hope. Writing of these encounters helps the diarist comprehend these lines from Gerard Manley Hopkins:

The world is charged with the grandeur of God.

It will flame out, like shining from shook foil.

Writing Our Bible

All religions spring from a real person's religious experience, whether Abraham, Moses, Jesus, or Mohammed. Religion— a tradition of worship and wisdom— is rooted in those experiences of individuals, which later were told in stories. Belief, whether it's in the teachings of the Bible, the Koran, or the Buddha, flows from the stories remembered and told from one generation to another.

Diaries, journals, and memoirs provide windows into the divine activity and revelation in people's lives. In this way, as they write their journals, people compose their own Bible or book, their own salvation history or sacred story. Marion Woodman remarks, "Journaling, I listen to my own soul and dance my life with the divine at its center. . . . The journal [is] the sacred place in which we dialogue with our own

"Sanity proclaims that immediate awareness is simply a state of appreciation. . . . **Immediate awareness** is the clear clean air without which healing and growth are stunted."

Gerald May

"The very act of **story telling**... is by definition **holy**.... We tell stories because we can't help it. We tell stories because we love to entertain and hope to edify. We tell stories because they **fill the silence** death imposes. We tell stories because they save us."

James Carroll

unconscious and hear the bubbling up of our own sacred springs."

While writing honestly in the journal, a person is, in fact, doing narrative theology: Theologian Martin Marty calls narrative theology "talking about God by telling stories of humans." Light is all around and inside every human being. The workings of the Spirit are all around and inside each human heart. The journal helps the writers look, listen, pay attention, reflect, and grow wise out of the conversations they have with a loved one, the conflicts they feel while making a decision, the grief they experience over the death of a dog-companion.

In one of his memoirs, *The Sacred Journey*, Frederick Buechner records his conviction that each day holds the promise of encounters with the Holy One and that by writing of these, the diarists does tell a sacred story:

There is no chance thing through which God cannot speak—even the walk from the house to the garage that you have walked ten thousand times before, even the moments when you cannot believe there is a God who speaks at all anywhere. He speaks, I believe, and the words he speaks are incarnate in the flesh and blood of our selves and of our own footsore and sacred journeys. . . . He says he is with us on our journeys. He says he has been with us since each of our journeys began. Listen for him. Listen to the sweet and bitter airs of your present and your past for the sound of him.

The Bible tells the story of God's actions in the life of the Israelites. The Ramayana tells the story of the pantheon of Hindu deities. Individuals can tell the story of the Spirit in their lives through the diary.

In another place, Buechner comments, "All theology, like all fiction, is at its heart autobiography, and . . . what a theologian is doing essentially is examining as honestly as he[she] can the rough and tumble of his[her] own experience with all its ups and downs, its mysteries and loose ends." As diarists examine their experiences and form convictions, they deepen their spirituality and their sense of the sacred in their story. In effect, they are writing their Bible. Journal writing is a sacred task. Over the millennia the practice has blessed the serious writer with its wisdom.

chapterthree

StartingtoWrite

"No matter what the writing task, if I **search my soul** and **my heart** I will find a way to capture some kind of energy, to somehow bring down **a little fire** to **change myself.**"

David Bradley

Writing Over the Edge

C lasses on journal or memoir writing often open with a simple writing activity. Instructors tell their class something like this: "With pen in hand and blank paper in front of you, write a spontaneous, one-page autobiography. For purposes of the exercise, don't organize your thoughts before you start. Just pick up your pen and begin writing. Once you begin, do not take your pen off the page until you have completed the one-page autobiography. Please, begin! When you finish, read what you wrote. Note any surprises, pieces of the story that might surprise you for appearing on the page."

Writing this simple, one-page autobiography might or might not have uncovered any surprises. Chances are, though, that as the writers pondered this short piece of writing, something in the piece is cause for wonder. Why did Aunt Gert appear there? Why did I start by talking about our mutt, Trixie? And so on. Journal writers write, in part, because the process is in itself an adventure in discovering, as Frost says, "something I didn't know I knew," or remembered or felt strongly about.

When we write, we always write over the edge of our consciousness. On starting a new notebook, novelist Edith Wharton said: "Perhaps at last I shall be able to write down some disconnected thoughts, old and new—gather together the floating scraps of experience that have lurked for years in corners of my mind." Wharton's description of what happens when we write in our journal or diary resonates with anyone who has taken to this practice. Writing inevitably brings up topics, images, memories, and feelings that we have stored away in our unconscious. If we write freely and honestly, spontaneously and playfully, they bubble up from the pool of our unconscious.

In *The Writing Life*, award-winning author, Annie Dillard describes what happens this way: "When you write, you lay out a line of words. The line of words is a miner's pick, a woodcarver's gouge, a surgeon's probe. You wield it, and it digs a path you follow. Soon you find yourself deep in new territory." Often the "new territory" is actually unfinished business from our past, strong feelings about the present that we refuse to let ourselves really consider, and wonderful ideas for the future.

Writing sorts through all the pieces of our experience, lays them on a page, and allows us to see them clearly—often for the first time. Frequently patterns in the pieces begin to emerge and make sense. We always say more about who we are, what we feel, and what we are about than we know when we first put pen to paper. Thus, writing regularly leads to discoveries. That is what makes it such an exciting, sometimes even scary, adventure.

Writing helps us sort through our lives and discover hidden truths about the lived experience of our beliefs, the truths hidden in the business of our lives and behind the masks that we wear in our family, our workplace, our church, temple, mosque, or synagogue, and our community. A diary is a place in which we can be totally honest with ourselves, something we want to be deep down.

> "You must be a great **warrior** when you contact **first thoughts** and **write** from them."
>
> *Natalie Goldberg*

Our Companion

It's no surprise that many journal writers have given names to their diaries. Anne Frank called her diary, Kitty. Zlata Filipovic called hers Mimmy. Some diarists address their reflections to God, while others just start with "Dear Diary." No matter. The journal becomes a friend, a confidant, a healing listener, and a wise counselor.

Keeping a journal is like holding a long, interesting conversation with a trusted friend who keeps us company. Company comes from two Latin words, *com* and *panis*, which mean "with" and "bread." When we talk with someone, we nurture each other like two people sharing bread. According to Marlene Schiwy, "Your journal is the most readily transportable, the most accommodating and forgiving companion you will ever have!" A journal companion won't forget and spill the beans to another friend, and the diarist won't have to buy an extra plane ticket to take this companion on vacation.

In our conversation, we learn new things. Some of what we learn is about ourselves. In a wonderful way, the diary is our true self, the self that at a deep level we are before the Creator. By writing these letters to our spirit, we are engaged in meditation—awareness, a long, loving look at the real. Thus, as discussed in chapter 1, we emerge more whole, freer of the unconscious forces that push and pull us, and more in tune with who we are truly called to be.

Courage

Bette Davis said that growing old wasn't for sissies. The same could be said for writing a diary or journal. Doris Grumbach, who no one would call

"The daily writing was where and how I worked towards a re-integration of the **aspects of Self** which had been fragmented. So it was a search, a quest, to find the pieces and then a long process of **writing them into a whole** I could live with."

Elly Danica

a sissy, declared in her journal: "Keeping a journal thins my skin. I feel open to everything, aware, charged by the acquisition of interesting (to me) entries, hypersensitive to whatever I hear, see, guess, read, am told. Matters that once might have gone unnoticed are no longer lost on me. I may sue my publisher for not providing me with sufficient protection against assault by whatever sensations are out there." Grumbach is, of course, correct.

Writing opens our awareness to the outside and inside worlds. When we open our eyes and hearts, we may see and feel things that we have shoved into our unconscious for a long time. Anne Frank announced in her famous diary: "I want to write, but more than that, I want to bring out all kinds of things that lie buried deep in my heart." Bringing out all kinds of things that have been buried in our hearts is healing, freeing, but also revealing, challenging, and sometimes frightening.

In *A Writer's Diary,* Virginia Woolf confided:

> What sort of diary should I like mine to be? Something loose knit and yet not slovenly, so elastic that it will embrace any thing, solemn, slight or beautiful that comes into my mind. I should like it to resemble some deep old desk, or capacious hold-all, in which one flings a mass of odds and ends without looking. I should like to come back, after a year or two, and find that the collection had sorted itself . . . into a mould, transparent enough to reflect the light of our life.

Journal writing helps writers sort life out and hold it "transparent" to the light. This is a positive step to growth and enlightenment, but often not easy. So, journaling isn't for sissies. Worth it, yes. Comfortable, not always.

Varieties of Writing for the Soul

There is a variety of personal writing that helps the diarist get started. Inevitably the differences of approach may blur in the process of writing. All of these types of writing are ultimately *memoir*, that is: personal, written reflections on events.

The Diary: Diaries have traditionally been the most personal of soul-growing writing. They are usually composed daily and record events of that one day. They are personal records and are not intended to be read by others or to be published. Indeed, blank diaries sold in bookstores or stationary shops often come complete with lock and key. Anne Frank's diary survived,

"I must write it all out, at any cost. Writing is thinking. It is more than living, for it is being conscious of living."

Anne Morrow Lindbergh

but clearly was not meant to be seen by others. This is typical of diarists.

Most diarists would agree with Sheila Bender when she says this about keeping a diary: "Each piece of experience builds into a bigger piece of experience. When you report where you are, what you see, taste, touch, feel, and smell, you also release what is inside of you, the pattern of what you have learned."

The Journal: "Journal" and "diary" are often used interchangeably. "Diary" became closely associated with young girls writing to "Dear Diary" and so the term seemed to some too childlike for adults to use. In any case, in the story of personal writing, journal keeping took on a somewhat more formal meaning. Journals were often kept as immediate records of events for later reference. Some journals were published and became public records and important sources for historians. *The Journals of Lewis and Clark* are a good example of this. After months of careful, largely dispassionate record keeping, on November 7, 1805, they made this entry:

> Great joy in camp. We are in view of the ocean . . . this great Pacific Ocean which we been so long anxious to see, and the roreing or noise made by the waves brakeing on the rockety shores (as I suppose) may be heard distictly.

Lewis and Clark's journal offers a record of their adventure. It has been a source of inspiration and historical information ever since.

But every person's life can be an adventure, even if they never leave town. Writers who sincerely follow and reflect on their inner journey are recording their own voyage of discovery. Novelist and journal writer May Sarton certainly experienced journal writing this way: "I feel happy to be keeping a journal again. I've missed it, missed naming things as they appear, missed the half hour when I push all duties aside and savor the experience of being alive in this beautiful place."

The Log: Logs are more formal still. Scientists keep logs of their experiments. Ships' captains keep logs of their voyages, noting distances covered, latitude and longitude, and so on. Even so, psychologist Ira Progoff who developed journal writing into a powerful therapeutic tool used the term "log" to refer to intimately personal writing in his "intensive journal" process.

Autobiography: The term "autobiography" often connotes the complete story of someone's life from birth to death. In fact, most autobiographies are only partial accounts. In any case, many autobiographies have their bases in journals or diaries. Even when they do not, they are composed of personal reflections and stories, the telling of which has all the benefits described by writing diaries or journals.

10 Commandments for
Journal Keeping

Teachers of journal writing and practiced diarists would generally agree with these suggestions:

1. *Try to write every day, or at least regularly.* Even if a person cannot spend a great deal of time writing, if they simply get down a few lines the habit will develop. They can describe one event, remind themselves of one blessing of the day. Writing consistently "plants the act" of writing that will grow into a habit.

2. *Choose a handy, comfortable notebook.* Journals come in all sizes. Some have lines and others don't. A diarist can buy journals with fancy covers or use spiral notebooks bought at a dollar store. I like to use spiral notebooks of 5-by-7 3/4 inches or 5 1/2 by 8 1/2 inches; they are inexpensive, portable, and with 80 sheets will last a long time. For many years, my main journal has been a 5 1/2-by-8 1/2-inch three-ring notebook with a 1-inch spine. This way I can keep adding new sheets of paper as I need them. Having pockets in the covers can be a nice feature, too.

A word about journaling on computer: I have a friend who suffers from neuropathy in her fingers, the results of rheumatoid arthritis; she cannot hold a pen very long, so she journals on the computer. Others just find it natural and comfortable. On the other hand, many of us use computers all day for our work. Consequently, intimate writing of the journal just seems harder to do on the computer. Also, we might not want to take our hardware on a canoe trip or in our backpack.

Journal writing should be personal, convenient, and intimate, whether on a computer or in a notebook. Anaïs Nin, most of whose published writings were her journals, describes just such a playful, versatile journal practice: "What an ambulant diary. At times behind desks, under a mattress, in an unlit stove, in trunks, in valises, iron boxes, buses, subways, taxis, lecture-hall desks, briefcases, in doctors' offices, hospital waiting rooms, park benches, on café tables, hair-dressers' salons. The pages often stained with coffee, wine, tears, lipstick."

"The writing process alchemically alters me, leaving me transformed. . . . Written words change us all and make us more than we could ever be without them."

Bell Hooks

3. *Write in pen.* Pencil smudges and can make future references to the journal difficult. But many journal keepers like to have some colored pens ready in case they want to draw or decorate.

4. *Date all entries.* This practice helps the diarist find entries if they later wish to.

5. *Recall the audience.* Unless writers decide otherwise, they are writing to themselves and, depending on their belief, their Higher Power. Recalling that only they and their God are the audience should free writers to open their heart and mind completely.

6. *Before writing, take a few deep breaths and relax.* The process of writing in itself can be relaxing, but slowing down for a few minutes before beginning can open mind and heart.

7. *Exile censors.* Whenever we write, some of us have inner censors that immediately begin correcting our spelling, critiquing our style, and sneering at our penmanship. Other censors might say, "You can't say that!" or "What would your husband think if he knew you thought that!" While keeping a journal, we should usher our censors out of the door. When writing the journal, diarists can ignore the rules of

grammar, political correctness, or politeness. This is a place to let it rip and be boldly blunt.

8. *Be descriptive, not judgmental.* Sometimes when we write, we tend to short circuit our full experience by saying things like, "It was a good day" or "It was a lousy day" and leaving it at that. For journal writing to be freeing, diarists try instead to describe what happened, who they met, where they went, how they felt; what made the day good or lousy. Description like this helps writers gain a more complete sense of their life. In the process they might just find that what they had called a "lousy day" may have had hidden blessings that were only uncovered as they were described.

9. *Write, write, and write some more.* Just write. Then write some more. That is the most important "commandment" for journal writers. While this book and other books on journal or memoir writing will suggest many topics about which to write and techniques for writing, anything can be written in the journal. Most important for the journal to be healing and freeing is that it is honest and spontaneous.

10. *Finally, keep the journal in a safe place, even under lock and key.* A journal belongs to the writer—period. No one—*no one*—has a right to read it, unless the writer gives her or him permission. Insecurity about the safety of the journal will stifle a diarist's ability to be thoroughly frank.

Tried and True Practices

Underlying most approaches to journal writing are the following techniques. Journal keepers use them, especially when they feel stuck. Some diarists write every entry as a letter. Other journal writers simply date their entries and then flow write. These and the other techniques in subsequent chapters can be described as a journal writing toolbox. The diarist can pick out just the right tool when a problem presents itself.

> # "Writing has got to be an act of discovery....
> ## I write to find out what I'm thinking about."
>
> *Edward Albee*

Flow or free writing. This is probably the most common way of journaling. Science fiction writer Ray Bradbury describes what happens when we flow write: "The faster your blurt, the more swiftly you write, the more honest you are. In hesitation is thought. In delay comes the effort for a style, instead of leaping upon truth which is the *only* style worth deadfalling or tiger-trapping." Free writing is just what it says: writing quickly, spontaneously, and freely about whatever comes to mind, allowing feelings and ideas to flow out uncensored and unchecked.

Free writing can be done for any amount of time. Some people like to actually set a timer to write steadily for 10, 20, or 30 minutes. Others free write every morning until they have filled some pages. To benefit most from free writing, diarists read what they wrote, note any uncovered treasures, and write down how they feel. Even when he was a homeless, alcoholic nomad, Timothy E. Donohue dated his entries, wrote regularly—though sometimes he was either too drunk to write or lost his pen, he stuck with it. Eventually, the University of Chicago Press published Donohue's *In the Open: Diary of a Homeless Alcoholic.* Some instinct that the journal was important made Donohue preserve it. The entire volume was written in this stream of consciousness flow-writing:

Friday February 1990 Yesterday, after writing the diary, I walked across the street from the library to a Circle K store, bought a quart of Pabst beer, and drank it in a nearby park as a prelude to a lunch of hot dogs and ice-cream sandwiches. In the evening I bought a half-pint of brandy but drank only about half of it before eating chicken and canned beets at my campsite out in the desert. These minor episodes of drinking were mostly intended to ease the discomfort of a hangover from drinking more than two liters of white wine the day before. It will be interesting to discover, as the days go by, whether erecting this "window into my soul" by chronicling my daily use and the feelings attendant on that use will mitigate the habit or perhaps eliminate it altogether.

If you get stuck, write a word or phrase over and over until something else comes out of the pen. Try to keep your pen on the paper, writing continuously, because once you hesitate you start thinking instead of just letting the words tumble out onto the page.

Journal writing didn't cure Donohue of his alcoholism, but as the free writing entries continued he began to understand and confront himself.

This is one of the best techniques for making discoveries and uncovering buried treasures. Then, as these discoveries are made, the writer can use one of the other approaches described here to explore the discovery even further.

Lists. Another tried and true journal technique is making lists. Again, Ray Bradbury supplies helpful direction: "I began to make lists of titles. . . . These lists were the provocations, finally, that caused my better stuff to surface. . . . If you are a writer, or would hope to be one, similar lists, dredged out of the lopside of your brain, might well help you discover *you*, even as I flopped around and finally found me." Writing lists is a type of brainstorming and can trigger further exploration of each item listed. Lists can provide an outline for further writing.

"List" comes from "listen." Writing lists is just another way of listening to our inner spirit. As we write, our spirit is given voice. As Bradbury suggests, each item on our list can form the title of a whole story from our life. Making lists is especially useful when we are rushed for time, but want to write. In fact, it is so useful that we'll apply this tool to other techniques discussed in the following chapters.

As with flow writing, diarists seek to write their lists quickly and spontaneously. Any list topic can help a writer generate memories of connected events and ideas, which in turn can lead to further exploratory writing. Natalie Goldberg in her book *Writing Down the Bones* suggests: "Making a list is good. It makes you start noticing material for writing in your daily life, and your writing comes out of a relationship with your life and its texture." Another nice thing about making lists is that they can be written anywhere in short bursts of energy.

Letters—usually unsent. Sometimes we just need to pour out our feelings—anger, joy, frustration, happiness, grief, or a mixture of all these—to someone. The "recipient" may be dead or alive but unreceptive. Or the unsent letter may simply let us release pent up feelings so that we can calm down and then write a letter that can actually be sent.

Unsent letters invite us to say anything to anyone, even to God. Also, unsent letters give us an audience with which to communicate. In Alice Walker's powerful novel, *The Color Purple*, Celie, an abused, poor woman, writes her letters to God because she has no one else who will listen. If we need to say something from the heart to someone, but cannot say it directly, an unsent letter may be a useful approach to take.

For instance, if a diarist had listed "all the people who love you," reviewing the list might help the writer remember a long lost relationship and perhaps some unfinished business with the person. To come to some understanding of the issues in the relationship or to express regrets or hopes, the diarist could write an unsent letter, expressing what is in her or his heart. Or, maybe the writer would compose an unsent letter to God, telling God what's in her or his mind and heart these days.

Spiral writing. In her book, *A Voice of Her Own*, Marlene Schiwy suggests that we can follow up a period of free writing by pulling out one sentence or idea that pops out of the free writing as somehow important. She says, "Rewrite it at the top of a new page. That becomes the first sentence in your next round of writing. Repeat this process three or four times, as often as you like." Spiral writing is a handy way of fleshing out and digging deeper into a topic simply touched on or briefly described in flow writing.

Dialogue Writing. A dialogue is going on inside our head even as we flow write. We write in response to some internal question buzzing in our brain. Most writing comes from a reaction to a question. Stating questions explicitly and then answering them in writing can help us clarify our thinking and get a fix on our feelings. In writing a dialogue we start seeing two sides of an issue, and we put ourselves in another pair of shoes. We take both sides of a conversation to gain empathy and comprehension of two points of view.

Before entering the dialogue, writers want to usher their censors to the door and remember to write down whatever comes to mind. The dialogue can be written in a play format, for example:

Me: Why do you make me so angry?

John: Let's face it, we're polar opposites.

Me: Like how opposites?

Many people, for instance, like to write dialogues with someone they have recently been in conflict with.

"We can avoid looking directly at issues for a long time while writing in monologue, but dialogue gets to the heart of the matter."

Christina Baldwin

> "For me the initial **delight** is in the **surprise** of remembering something I didn't know **I knew.**"
>
> *Robert Frost*

If they start with a question and then let the other person speak his or her truth back, continue to talk about the issues between them until they're done, the writer may reach a clearer and more empathetic understanding of the other person's point of view. In any relationship, each party is only 50 percent of the experience. Dialogue writing can help the diarist delve into the other 50 percent. If writers take time to ponder the experience, they often gain new and helpful insights.

Set Out

As we journal we are constructing and recording the book of our life. Courage is required because we never know what lies ahead, but as Joan Baez remarked, "You don't get to choose how you're going to die. Or when. You can only decide how you're going to live. Now." The journal is a way of leaning into life, befriending it, and finding its miracles.

Flow writing, lists, unsent letters, spiral writing, and dialogues are five basic journaling techniques. Each of the following chapters will introduce other means of making journal writing a true voyage of discovery.

chapterfour

WhereAreYOU?

"**Miracles seem to rest,** not so much upon faces or voices or healing power coming suddenly near to us from far off, but upon our perceptions being made finer so that **for a moment our eyes** can **see** and our **ears hear** that which is about us always."

Willa Cather

Adam and Eve, Where Are You?

The story of Eve, Adam, the serpent, and the forbidden tree is a familiar one. However, the full significance of the story—like all good stories—keeps emerging after many readings and close reflection. After Adam and Eve had eaten the fruit of the tree, they go off and try to hide from God, whom they hear walking in the garden. They know that they have done something wrong. As they crouch in the bushes, God calls out to them, "Where are you?" Now that may seem like a strange question coming from an all-knowing God, a God who clearly knew where they were.

The Jewish philosopher Martin Buber offers a wonderful insight into the story:

Adam hides himself to avoid rendering accounts, to escape responsibility for his way of living. Every man hides for this purpose, for every man is Adam [every woman Eve] and finds himself in Adam's situation. . . . This situation can be precisely defined as follows: Man cannot escape the eye of God, but in trying to hide from him, he is hiding from himself. True, in him too there is something that seeks him, but he makes it harder and harder for that "something" to find him. This question is designed to awaken man and destroy his system of hideouts; it is to show man to what pass he has come and to awaken in him the great will to get out of it.

Before we can live more freely and more wisely, we need to honestly answer God's question to Adam and Eve: "Where are you?" God knows, but often *we* don't.

"Where am I?" stands as a key spiritual question, not just in Judaism or Christianity. Hinduism has a story that goes like this. A pilgrim arrived in a holy city and began searching for a *guru* to open the secrets of spiritual growth for him. His search was proving futile. At last he asked a long-time resident of the city, "Where can I find a *guru*? They all seem to have gone missing." The citizen scratched his beard, thought about it, and finally told the man to follow him. His guide led the man to the grounds of a temple and introduced him to a wise, ascetic, ancient man. The pilgrim asked, "I have been looking for days for all the *guru*s that I was told lived in the city. Where are they?" The *guru* shook his head and replied, "Oh, pilgrim, that is not the question at all." Bewildered the pilgrim replied, "What do you mean?" Looking at the pilgrim, the *guru* said, "The question is not 'Where are all the *gurus?*' The question is, 'Where are *you?*'"

If we wish to grow spiritually, we need to steadily ask this hard question or versions of it. Where am I? Is who I am inside, the same person I seem on the outside? How conscious am I of where I really am? Am I conscious of all that I really am, or do I live on automatic pilot? Have I worn my masks so long that I have forgotten my true self? Is this person I project who I really am?

In *An Interrupted Life: The Diaries of Etty Hillesum, 1941–1943*, Etty Hillesum records in her journal her answers to the questions just posed. She knew that time was against her. The Nazis had invaded her country and had begun sending Jews like her to concentration camps. With what time she had left, she wanted to confront the reality of her life. And so she writes:

Sunday, 9 March [1941]. Here goes, then. This is a painful and well-nigh insuperable step for me: yielding up so much that has been suppressed to a blank sheet of lined paper. The thoughts in my head are sometimes so clear and so sharp and my feelings so deep, but writing about them comes hard. The main difficulty, I think, is a sense of shame. So many inhibitions, so much fear of letting go, of allowing things to pour out of me, and yet that is what I must do if I am ever to give my life a reasonable and satisfactory purpose. . . . I am blessed enough intellectually to be able to fathom most subjects, to express myself clearly on most things; I seem to be a match for most of life's problems, and yet deep down something like a tightly-wound ball of twine binds me relentlessly and at times I am nothing more or less than a miserable, frightened creature, despite the clarity with which I can express myself.

> **"I not only have my secrets, I am my secrets."**
>
> *Frederick Buechner*

Asking the questions and confronting the realities she does can be scary, but healing and freeing as well. After all, before a wound can heal, we need to be aware of it, really look at it, diagnose it, and then tend to it. Psychologist Carl Rogers declared, "The curious paradox is that when I accept myself just as I am, then I can change." Too often we let hurts go, and then the healing takes longer and is more difficult. Like a person who lets a breast lump alone too long, truths we ignore can kill us spiritually.

Write!

To begin answering the question, "Who am I?" start by composing this autobiographical poem of seven lines:

Line 1: Write, I am (your first name)

Line 2: Write three self-describing words

Lines 3-6: Complete each of these sentences

I love

I hate

I am afraid

I wish

Line 7: Write your last name.

Accepting the True Self

These two stories from Judaism may help us understand and accept our true self. The renowned though humble Rabbi Bunam had grown blind in his old age. Nevertheless, sensing that some of his followers wished otherwise for him, he told them: "I should not like to change places with our father Abraham. What good would it do God if Abraham became like a blind Bunam, and blind Bunam became like Abraham? Rather than have this happen, I think I shall try to become a little more like myself."

"Write about things that are close to the nose."

William Carlos Williams

The second story is about the final words of Rabbi Zusya. Knowing that he was taking his last breaths, his followers asked him if he had any final wisdom to share with them. Zusya's eyes opened and, taking a deep breath, he said, "In the world to come, I will not be asked, Why were you not Moses? I will be asked, Why were you not Zusya?"

Each of us can only be who *we* are. The Creator made us to be who we are, not who someone else is. Surely we can learn from others and be inspired by their teaching and example. Nevertheless, if we accept the fact that we are made in the divine image, then we are called to be that divine image as we are. One description of our true self is this: the unique image of God that I am.

Unfortunately, most of us learn early on in life that somehow we are not enough. We are not smart enough, or tall enough, or thin enough, or witty enough, or patient enough, and, well, just not enough. So instead of developing our intelligence, making the best use of our height, learning how to be healthy, and so on, we are tempted to imitate "idols," to grind our teeth in envy, to hide, or to languish in bitter self-recrimination. Not a pleasant way to live.

Healthy self acceptance can begin with an honest account of all our gifts and all our challenges, all our light and all our shadows. Wilkie Au and Noreen Cannon tell us that "spiritual transformation consists in two movements: self-appropriation and self-transcendence. Self-appropriation involves self-knowledge and self-understanding. Practically, it means knowing what is going on inside ourselves: knowing who we are, knowing why we choose what we choose, why we do what we do and what our feelings and desires are." Thus, writing honest answers to these questions, which all come back to "Where am I?", can be a valuable tool in self-appropriation and spiritual transformation.

Self-appropriation includes a relentless but kindly look at our beliefs and actions. It looks at the light we shed and our hidden shadows. Those aspects of ourselves that we don't like to admit to, talk about, have exposed, and certainly don't accept are our "shadow." Another way of identifying our shadow is that it is the parts of who we are that stand in conflict with the ways in which we want to view ourselves.

We all have shadows, but they are not the enemies we think they are. My dad was good at keeping his profound affection in the shadows: that is until he had to give our dog away because of a move to a new assignment. After leaving Trixie with a loving family, my dad drove to the end of the long driveway and broke into sobs. This was the first and only time my mother ever saw him cry. I remember this story even now, forty years later, because somehow it makes my stoic, Germanic dad much more approachable and, even though I loved him, more lovable. I've often wondered how much energy he wasted hiding his tender heart in his shadow. When I have experienced this same

"The unawakened mind tends to make war against the way things are. . . . **War's roots are in ignorance.** Without understanding, we can easily become frightened."

Jack Kornfield

reluctance to show my emotions, remembering my dad has helped me bring my emotions out of the shadows. I believe that I am better for it, too.

The journal is a safe place for us to bring our hidden treasures out of the shadows. Yes, our shadows hold treasures: whether that is more powerful sexual energy than we care to admit, anger at a deceased parent, sensitivity to beauty, or fear of various kinds. Each of these "shadows" is part of our unique image of the divine; each shadow has energy that can be transformed when we appropriate it and accept it.

We worry about and fear most what we don't know. Journal writing helps us know "what we didn't know we knew," as Frost says.

Write!

Here are some lists that can help you discover where you are right now:

Compliments people often pay you

Favorite gifts or talents you have

Things that make you laugh

Worries that steadily bother you

Points about yourself that you least like

Things that make you fearful on a regular basis

Quotes you use all the time

Epitaphs that you would appreciate having on your grave marker

Beliefs and Actions

Two key parts of anyone's spirituality are (1) beliefs and (2) actions. To deepen their awareness of their spirituality, diarists need to explore their beliefs and their lived experience or actions taken.

> "The larger the island of knowledge, the greater the shoreline of wonder."
>
> *Ralph Stockman*

A Hindu sacred book, *The Bhagavad Gita*, says, "Humans are made by their beliefs. As they believe, so they are." Much contemporary research and experience would back this up. After all, what we believe is our "creed," which comes from a Latin word meaning "heart." So our beliefs or creed are "what we set our heart on."

John Wesley, founder of Methodism and missionary, explored the relationship between his beliefs and his actions in his journal:

> Tuesday 24 [1738]: . . . I went to America to convert the Indians, but, oh, who shall convert me? Who, what, is he that will deliver me from this evil heart of unbelief? I have a fair summer

religion. I can talk well, nay, and believe myself, while no danger is near. But let death look me in the face, and my spirit is troubled. Nor can I say, *to die is gain.*

> "I have a sin of fear, that when I've spun My last thread, I shall perish on the shore!"

I think, verily, if the Gospel be true, I am safe, for I not only have given and do give all my goods to feed the poor . . . but I follow after charity (though not as I ought, yet as I can) if haply I may attain it. I *now* believe the Gospel is true. *I show my faith by my works* by staking my all upon it.

Like Wesley, by listing and exploring our beliefs—where our heart is—we can arrive at a fuller understanding of where we are. By knowing where we are in our beliefs, we have a chance at renewing, and maybe reforming, our spirituality.

faith

Write!

Periodically, journal writers find it renewing to write their own creed. This is done simply by writing lists of beliefs you hold about key areas of your life. If you say only what comes from your heart—not what you think you should say, a personal creed will emerge on the page that lays out where you are.

Here are statements you can begin your lists with:

About my relationships, I believe. . .

About God or Higher Power, I believe. . .

About work, I believe . . .

About the environment, I believe . . .

About my body, I believe . . .

About sexuality, I believe . . .

About religion, I believe . . .

After writing a creed or statement of beliefs, writers trying to describe the state of their spirituality next need to examine their actions. Shakyamuni Buddha once told his followers: "My actions are my only true belongings. I cannot escape the consequences of my actions. My actions are the ground on which I stand." Actions are indeed "the ground on which we stand." The Buddha knew that. Jesus knew that. And we certainly know it too. Talk is indeed cheap, and our actions speak louder than words. Cliches, but true. Our beliefs are one part of our spirituality, our actions the other part. So, in order to understand where we are, reviewing our actions over the most recent period of our life is essential.

To explore their actions, journal writers periodically spend periods thoroughly examining how they behave. Pose these and other questions to yourself and write your honest answers:

- How have I been involved in or taken part in relationships with significant people in my life, in social groupings, in political events?

- How have I been engaged with God or my Higher Power?

- What actions have I taken at work, what key decisions made?

- How have I interacted with the environment?

- What actions have I taken in regard to my body-self?

- ➻ What have been my experiences of my sexuality?

- ➻ How have I been engaged in expressing my religious involvement?

- ➻ What other key moments, memorable actions, important decisions have I experienced over this most recent period of my life?

"Birth is not one act; it is a process. . . . To live is to be born every minute. Death occurs when birth stops."

Erich Fromm

Having written such lists and reflected on "the lived experience" of this most recent period of their lives, most diarists will see patterns. Any strong reactions that an event or events raise for them are clues that these moments held special significance.

Henri J.M. Nouwen was a renowned spiritual writer known for the sometimes brutal honesty about himself that he shared in his writings. In *The Genesee Diary: Report from a Trappist Monastery*, Nouwen confronts the disharmony between his beliefs and actions:

During the afternoon I worked with Brother Brian in Salt Creek looking for granite stones for the new church. . . .

The whole afternoon I was struggling with the old question: Why didn't I really enjoy the work, and why did I want to go back to my books to read about the spiritual life? Is selecting stones in the creek bed not the best spiritual life possible? Why do I always want to read *about* the spiritual life and not really live it? Brian was so quiet and content, and I so restless and impatient.

Such questions raised in the journal plant the seeds of renewal and transformation.

Write!

Clustering, webbing, or mind mapping may be especially helpful in tracing where you are in life.

1. In clustering, start by writing a subject that you want to explore in the middle of a blank page; draw a circle around it.

2. Then draw a line to some idea, memory, word, or feeling, write it down and circle it. If ideas are connected to that idea, draw lines out from it, write the idea or word, and circle it.

3. When a line of ideas runs out, go back to the central word and start another strand, looking for connections and other concepts.

4. To use this exercise in understanding the question, "Where am I?" write your first name in the middle of the blank sheet and begin webbing or clustering ideas, feelings, adjectives, and so on around it; let each of those words lead to other connections, and other connections. For example:

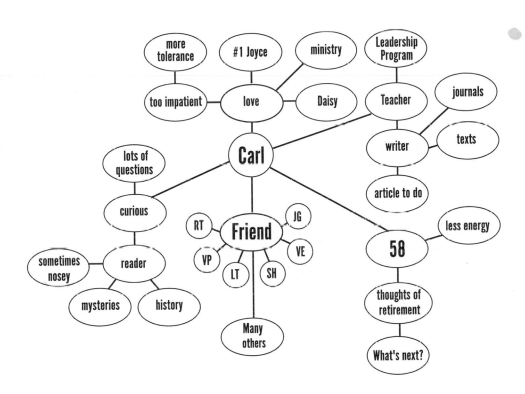

> "We are **the journey** itself. . . . The great rhythm of gain and loss is outside our control; what remains within our control is the **attitude** of willingness to find in even the bitterest losses what remains to be lived."
>
> *James Hollis*

Half Full, Half Empty

The whole project of writing our memoir is a journey of consciousness. Consciousness leads to choices: to honor or not to honor who we are right now, to appropriate and accept where we are or to deny and reject our place. Much depends on whether we feel compelled to judge and the lenses through which we see ourselves. Whether a glass is half empty or half full depends on our perceptions and choices, not on the glass. If we insist on judging our life as half-full or half-empty, we may be short-circuiting the first movement in spiritual transformation: self-appropriation.

In Lillian Hellman's journal, she certainly demonstrates the battle that can go on between seeing life as half full or half empty. As she examined the tensions in her life, she eventually worked through them, but on this day, the battle raged:

Budapest, April 30

Is it age, or was it always my nature, to take a bad time, block out the good times, until any success became an accident and failure seemed the only truth? I can't sleep, I have had a headache for three days, I lie on the bed telling myself that nothing has ever gone right, doubting even [Dashell] Hammett and myself, remembering how hard the early years sometimes were for us when he didn't care what he did or spoiled, and I didn't think I wanted to stay long with anybody, asking myself why, after the first failure, I had been so frightened of marriage, who the hell did I think I was alone in a world where women don't have much safety, and, finally, on the third night, falling asleep with a lighted cigarette and waking to a burn on my chest.

> "Everthing that happens to you is **your teacher.** The **secret** is to learn to sit at the feet of your own **life** and be taught by it."
>
> *Polly Berrien Berends*

Journaling like this is raw and tough, but Hellman and millions of other journal writers decide that it's worth it.

As we write the lists of our beliefs and actions, we probably spot numerous inconsistencies between what we believe and how we have acted—I sure have plenty of them in my lists. We might be tempted to discouragement, especially if we have bought into the notion that we have to be perfect. If this is the case, we can remind ourself of Jesus' rebuke of the disciple who called him "good": "Do not call me good. Only God is good."

The other way of looking at our writing about "where you are" is to simply invite all that we have written into our awareness. Simple awareness is the beginning of liberation. It is a great opportunity. This awareness can lift us into the second movement of spiritual transformation: self-transcendence. As we understand and accept ourselves just as we are, this enlightenment can invite us to move beyond where we are, to align our choices more closely with our beliefs, to listen more closely to the Spirit within us, to become more compassionate and loving. This is the true self.

So, once again—and this is a constant motif in the book—for journal writing to have its maximum benefit, we need to let go of judgments about the "goodness" or "badness" of where we are. We need not decide if the glass is half full or half empty. Instead, we can drink and appreciate the water, and let it refresh us, accept it as a gift for the journey.

Write!

These are some other exercises that you can use to explore where you are:

1. Write an unsent letter to your shadow(s): those parts of ourself which we try to hide or that conflict with the way we want to be seen. First greet the shadow(s) and then tell the shadow(s) what you know about them. Try to describe how you understand them.

2. Imagine that you are your best friend, and then write a letter to yourself describing yourself as your own best friend would.

3. Writing your responses to these questions opens new perceptions: What metaphors form in my mind when I feel the movement of my life right now? What images reflect the tone of my life? Is my life like a raging river tearing out trees from the shoreline? Is my life like a calm pool on a sunny day? If I close my eyes and relax, breathe deeply and slowly, what images and metaphors form. Write these images down.

"An **unconscious secret** is more injurious than a conscious one. . . to cherish secrets and hold back emotions is **a psychic misdemeanor** for which nature visits us with sickness."

C. G. Jung

Present Moment, Wonderful Moment

Answering the question "Where are you?" is not a journal writing activity that we need to do every day, but periodically—whether monthly, every two months or six months—it invites us to focus on the present period of our life. It is a particularly useful exercise when we feel at loose ends, out of focus, or overwhelmed by life. Progoff calls this sort of writing "the period log," others describe it as "the identity journal." In any case, this descriptive, non-judgmental writing can help us affirm the present moment as a wonderful moment.

Nearly two millennia ago, Emperor Marcus Aurelius wrote in his journal *Meditations*:

> Were you to live three thousand years or even

thirty thousand, remember that the sole life which a man can lose is that which he is living at the moment. . . . Man lives only in the present, in this fleeting instant: all the rest of his life is either past or gone, or not yet revealed.

This present time is what we have as our life. Journaling about our life at this present time helps us really live into it. The choice is ours.

In a small village, an old woman had gained the reputation of being a healer and having the ability to see into people's hearts. The villagers respected her and were grateful to her but also somewhat feared her powers. One day a group of village children decided to test the old woman. They didn't believe that anyone could be as wise and see into others' hearts as all the adults believed the old woman could. One of the children caught a baby bird that had fallen from the nest. Holding it in his hands, he told the others that he would test the old woman this way: "I'll ask

"Love the moment, and the energy of the moment will spread beyond all boundaries."

Corita Kent

"We need to remember that **where we are going** is here, that any practice is simply a means **to open our hearts** to what is in front of us."

Jack Kornfield

her if the bird is dead or alive. If she says it's alive, I'll crush it. If she says it's dead, I'll let it go." So the band of children caught up with the old woman in the village square. "Old woman," asked the boy with the baby bird hidden in his hands, "is this baby bird in my hands dead or alive?" The old woman looked steadily at the boy and then looked into the eyes of each child. Her eyes were alive in her wrinkled face. Finally, she turned the full power of her gaze upon the boy holding the baby bird and said, "The baby bird is in your hands."

Our life is in our hands. We can crush it or let it fly. Answering honestly the question "Where are you?" lets our spirit live.

Write!

If you periodically just relax, breathe deeply, recollect your recent life, then begin writing about the question "Where am I?" with an open heart, you can stay more in tune with who you are. If you allow your heart to speak and let your feelings surface, you will know the shape of your spirituality. Then you can make the choices that need to be made to move toward a richer, more harmonious life.

chapterfive

ADay'sJourney

"**Seeing** is of course very much a matter of verbalization. Unless I call my attention to what passes before my eyes, I simply won't see. . . . It's all a matter of **keeping my eyes open.**"

Annie Dillard

The Day's Story

Keeping a daily account of life is basic to the diary or journaling process. If a person never wrote about "where they are," as described in the last chapter, or never used the exercises in the remaining chapters, but kept the diary or daily journal, they would profit from journaling. It is the most basic form of spiritual writing. In this way, journal writers pay attention to or meditate on the daily lived experience of their beliefs. "The eye sees a great many things," as Thomas Edison said, "but the average brain records very few of them." The daily journal helps us record our experience.

There are many ways of paying attention to and telling the story of the day, that is, keeping the daily journal. Some diarists jot down the barest details. For example, between 1785–1812, Martha Ballard served as a midwife to her community in New England. During all these years she kept a diary in which she recorded the births attended, problems faced, and her own experiences at home. Each entry is brief, almost a kind of shorthand. She lists and states the facts of the day: who and what. Nevertheless, the total diary provides a vivid account of life for women and families during the period. For instance, here is an entry from January 15, 1706: "At [William Mathews]. Birth 4th. This is the 612th Birth I have attended at Since the year 1777. The first I assisted was the wife of Petton Warrin in

July 1778. Birth William Mathews dagt. XX." As terse as it is, this entry records facts about the community, the pride she has in all the births for which she was midwife, and her intimate knowledge of the families. In other entries, her brief remarks tell about what was on her mind and about her life:

> [January 1796] 17 At Mr Peter Clearks. Death of Timothy Page's infant.

> 18 At Mr Clearks & Stephen Hinkleys. Births 5th and 6th. Received of William Moore 7/ 10 1/2 as a reward. Birth Stephen Hinkleys son. Birth William Moores son. XX

> [May 1809] 23 Sowd spring peas.

> 24 At home. Workt in my gardin.

> 25 At James Catons. Birth 4th. Fell from my hors on my way home. Received 9/ at William Babcok. At James Caton's Birth. His 11th child, 5 son. XX.

Martha Ballard, like most other diary and journal writers, wanted to leave a record of her life, and she certainly used it to look back on what she had accomplished.

During the Civil War, Catholic priest Father James B. Sheeran managed to keep a journal of his experiences on the march with the Confederate Army. With more detail than Martha Ballard, he describes who he met, what happened during his day, but also his thoughts and feelings—among them strong Confederate convictions. While ministering to Stonewall Jackson's troops after one engagement in 1862, he wrote:

> Aug. 11 I spent the afternoon among the wounded prisoners we had carried from the field. . . . I devoted to the [northern] Capt. about an hour of my time during which I introduced him into a world of ideas altogether different from that in which he had hitherto been travelling. . . . [He maintained] that he was fighting only for preservation of the Constitution. My parting advice to him was this: "My very good man before going to bed every night try to recall to your memory the number of times Abe Lincoln has perjured himself by violating the Constitution since his introduction into office; then put your hand to your breast and ask yourself in the presence of God, if in fighting for your perjured President, you are fighting for the Constitution of your country."

Father Sheeran focuses his daily journal on what he did, but clearly he wants to record the fervor of his convictions. In doing so, his dairy throws harsh light on the reality that while Christianity abhors and condemns slavery today, it was not always so.

While taking care of her mother during her last illness, poet and novelist Madeleine L'Engle wrote a much more intimate daily journal that focuses on one key part of her life, her relationship with her mother and the experience of those last days. One of her entries describes a particularly poignant moment:

> I dress Mother in a fresh nightgown while Vicki and Janet finish with the bed. Most mornings, Mother hardly seems to notice what has happened, or to care. She will murmur, "I'm cold. I want to go back to bed"—she who used to be so fastidious, so sweet-smelling. But this morning as I sit with my arms around her while the girls ready the bed, she leans against me and, suddenly herself, she says, "Oh, darling, I'm so ashamed about everything."
>
> My heart weeps.

Clearly, L'Engle's diary reflects a vastly different story than Martha Ballard's or Father Sheeran's simply because where she is and what's going on is her story, not theirs. However, by simply describing what

"It's very strange, but the **mere act of writing** anything is a help. It seems to speed one on one's way."

Katherine Mansfield

happened, this entry in her journal provides a window for us and for her into her soul.

So, the first key to keeping the daily journal or diary is to get something, no matter how brief, down on paper about the day. The rest of this chapter and subsequent chapters provide direction about how diarists write reflections on the events of the day, but start with writing something down daily.

Write.

In her helpful book *Writing Down the Bones*, Natalie Goldberg advises, "Making a list is good. It makes you start noticing material for writing in your daily life, and your writing comes out of a relationship with your life and its texture." If we don't have time to write longer entries, listing can be a great way to keep a daily journal. Here are some lists to write in our diary or daily journal:

People to whom I showed kindness and love

People who showed me kindness and love

People with whom I had conflict

What made me sad

What made me laugh

Events that come immediately to mind and pen

Contributions I made to the planet today

Times when I was aware of the Holy

Blessings of the day

Stay Descriptive

In the daily journal, staying descriptive proves most helpful. Whether describing work, projects, feelings, insights, relationships, scenes, and so on, the very process of recording the events of the day will inevitably stir up further feelings, related ideas, and other issues. If journal writers feel the need to describe those other issues and feelings, fine, but description in the daily journal is valuable in and of itself as a starting place for further reflection if and when they wish to do so.

Description leads the writer into vision and revelation. The journal writer becomes a reporter whose whole job is telling one story: his or her own. In the diary, they record who, what, when, where, how. In the diary editorializing should be abandoned, though no diarist should get bent out of shape if they slip into that mode. Success in journaling is showing up to write. And while journaling, writers put their senses to work, telling about the sights, sounds, tastes, touches, and smells of the day.

"Every morning I awaken torn between the desire to save the world and the inclination to savor it."

E. B. White

Writers receive the most insight and release when they describe feelings with their proper names. If they are angry, they say they are angry. They tell what happened with the anger. When they have a moment of delight, they detail who, what, when, where, and how did the delight occur? When under a cloud, they describe what that cloud was about. Don't judge it and, please, don't censor it. What is, is. Best to become "fierce with reality."

In his advice about beginning to write, German poet Rainer Maria Rilke instructed: "Try, like some first human being, to say what you see and experience and love and lose. . . . Save yourself from general themes and seek those which your own everyday life offers you; describe your sorrows and desires, passing thoughts and the belief in some sort of beauty— describe all these with loving, quiet, humble sincerity, and use, to express yourself, the things in your environment." Rilke's advice is solid wisdom for diary writers. We know things when we give them their real names.

Lydia Allen Rudd's diary of her trip west in a covered wagon offers many good examples of descriptive writing and naming things:

> May 6 1852 Left the Missouri river for our long journey across the wild uncultivated plains. . . . As we left the river bottom and ascended the bluffs the view from them was handsome! In front of us as far as vision could reach extended the

green hills covered with fine grass. . . . About half a mile down the river lay a steamboat stuck fast on a sandbar. Still further down lay the busy village of St. Joseph looking us a good bye and reminding us that we were leaving all signs of civilised life for the present. But with good courage and not one sigh I mounted my pony (whose name by the way is Samy) and rode slowly on.

As the long journey to the west continued, her diary records encounters with fierce storms, wagon accidents in which children were crushed, parching thirst, her fears and joys. With a little imagination, one can ponder Lydia Rudd pulling out her diary with a grandchild on her lap and using the worn pages to tell the child about her adventure: who was with her, what happened and how, where they encountered herds of buffalo, and so on.

Telling the story of a day is best done as soon as possible. Ideally, entries are written right after something happens while the details are still fresh in consciousness. If that is impossible, writing the daily journal at the end of the day can certainly be effective. If one cannot write every day, he or she should not give up. Daily journal or diary keeping can be done after a couple of days or at the end of a week. Lydia Rudd couldn't write entries every day because of one thing or another, but she caught up when she could.

It is important to remember that the daily log describes interior events, too. Diarists benefit most when they record inner experience: sadness after an argument with a friend, grief over the death of a companion animal, or any inner movement of spirit.

"Put yourself in the **present.** This was my principle when I wrote the diary—to **write** the thing I felt most strongly about that day. Start there and that starts the whole unraveling, because that has **roots** in the past and it has branches **into** the future."

Anaïs Nin

Write!

Here is how Christina Baldwin describes free or flow writing in the daily journal: "Flow writing is practice in stream of consciousness, learning to trust that no matter where you start, words will come to you. . . . Flow writing reveals the mind's agenda underneath the busyness of surface thoughts." Most diary writers use flow writing as the basic form of keeping a daily journal.

Date your entry, put pen to paper and begin unwinding the flow of your day. If you get stuck or cannot even begin, start describing some object in the room where you are. This often opens the gates of your consciousness. Keep writing whatever comes. If a censor starts bugging you, tell him or her to move aside—in writing of course. Keep writing. Stop when you've written yourself out.

Daily Entries, Veins of Gold

The daily journal is the vein of gold mined for topics to explore in the other parts of the journal. Doris Grumbach makes this clear when she says, "What is it that drives us to examine matters of cosmic significance—birth, faith, suffering, injustice, dying, and death—but the intrusion into our daily lives of niggling irritations and petty trifles." As it is recorded, what at first may appear as "the niggling irritations and petty trifles" is often found to be a matter of import. These irritations and trifles may trigger vivid memories and powerful emotions that beckon the writer to follow them using other helpful techniques for journaling beyond the daily journal.

> **"I am** what is around **me."**
>
> *Wallace Stevens*

In his memoir, *A Room Called Remember*, Frederick Buechner echoes Doris Grumbach's insight: "Every once in a while, life can be very eloquent. You go along day to day not noticing very much, not seeing or hearing very much, and then all of a sudden, when you least expect it very often, something speaks to you with such power that it catches you off guard, makes you listen whether you want or not. Something speaks to you out of your own life with such directness that it is as if it calls you by name and forces you to look where you have not had the heart to look before, to hear something that maybe for years you have not had the wit or the courage to hear." First, we write the diary. If "something speaks to you out of your own [daily] life" then we can explore that vein of gold.

So, the diary or daily journal records the day and thereby honors immediate experience. In telling the day's story, we make discoveries and reveal our deep desires, our forgotten wisdom and defining moments. Author Jon Hassler had been teaching for many years. While his career as a teacher had its own rewards, his secret desire had been to publish his first novel, *Staggerford*, the story of a teacher. While he waited to hear about the book's fate, he continued to keep his daily journal. On September 5, 1976, Hassler wrote this entry:

> I got this telegram: CONGRATULATIONS. ATHENEUM PUBLISHERS TAKING STAGGERFORD. CALL ME FOR DETAILS. BEST HARRIET. My beloved agent. Actually, I didn't get the telegram. My son got it. I was in the middle of cleaning the cabin when he called and read it to me over the phone. I think I was shaking a rug when the phone rang. I was up there with a friend named Chuck, who was washing dishes. . . . When I hung up the phone, I shivered and Chuck grinned. . . . It was two in New York and Harriet would be returning from lunch. I would give her twenty minutes to get back to her desk. In the meantime, I shook the rest of the rugs

and dusted. . . ."Chuck, I don't know if I believe this." Chuck grinned. Chuck is one of the few people in Minnesota who realizes that speaking to the world via the printed word has been my lifelong dream. . . . I called Harriet. As I listened to the sounds of a dozen tiny circuits engaging themselves between Minnesota and Manhattan, it occurred to me that I didn't know how to pronounce Atheneum.

In describing this moment of joy, Hassler reveals the pent up hopes that he had been living with for a long time. In subsequent entries in his *Staggerford Journals*, he explored all that this moment meant to him. In journaling, one day's reality can be the beginning of the next truth's unveiling.

"Once I begin the **act of writing,** it all falls away— the view from the window, the tools, the talismans, and I am unconscious of myself . . . one's carping inner critics are silenced for a time . . . there is always a **surprise,** a **revelation.** During the act of writing, I have told myself something that I didn't know I knew."

Gail Godwin

Write!

Try this systematic way of daily log writing:

1. Take some deep breaths and relax. In the quiet of your memory and then on paper begin reviewing the day's events, recalling especially those moments that remain vivid. Record as many details as you can.

2. Let your feelings surface, any anxieties, hopes, and plans that took shape during the day. In other words, what was the emotional coloring of the day?

3. Write about what kind of relationships came along, and what they were like.

4. Without censoring, try to describe: What went on in your inner life today?

5. Then stop, relax again, and write about what feelings you have right now, how you felt while writing?

6. End by just sitting quietly, absorbing the day, and resting from it.

Note: Some diarists find concentrating on one aspect of their daily life to be very helpful, especially if they are dealing with specific issues. For example, a friend had been struggling to drop the weight that she had gained while pregnant. While taking care of her newborn and dealing with all her other responsibilities, she just could not seem to focus her energies on getting back to a healthier weight. A longtime journal writer, she abandoned the general daily log and concentrated on her body—what she was eating, her level of activity, and so on. Losing the weight still took a while, but the daily "body" journal helped. When she was back to an acceptable weight she returned to the daily journal. Other people focus their daily journals on specific issues for some period until a resolution or understanding emerges: for example, daily writing about a tough relationship, the adventures of a trip, coping with a medical condition, grief over the loss of a loved one, an important pending decision, feelings and ideas about a project, and so on. When some understanding is reached or decision made, then return to the general daily journal.

> "Life is denied by lack of **attention,** whether it be to cleaning windows or trying to **write a masterpiece."**
>
> *Nadia Boulanger*

The Spirit in the Day

As has been described, keeping the daily journal inevitably leads us into considerations and revelations about our spirituality—how we live our beliefs. Many diarists make these three questions the focus of their daily writing:

1. Have my actions and decisions today aligned with my beliefs?

2. How have I loved today?

3. How did I sense the presence of God or my Higher Power or Allah or The Holy One or the Ground of Being during the day? OR: What did I hear from the Spirit today?

Many diary keepers spend some time listing, flow writing, journaling using other questions, and then writing about these three questions. Others focus on just these three questions or some combination of them. In any case, by spending time with the questions we can discover the Spirit that may seem hidden in the bustle of our daily life.

Have my actions and decisions today aligned with my beliefs? We have discussed this question in the previous chapters. Clearly, if we are to stay whole or in harmony inside ourselves, our actions need to reflect our beliefs. Charting the relationship between our beliefs and actions each day gives us a consistent way of doing so.

How have I loved today? The cornerstone of human development and spiritual growth is loving wisely and well. Again, asking this question of ourselves at the end of a day brings us face to face with the reality of how we have loved one day at a time. As we examine in writing the answers to the question, we can let go of our failures, rejoice in our love, and choose to love again on the morrow.

How did I sense the presence of God or my Higher Power or Allah or The Holy One or the Ground of Being during the day? OR: What did I hear from the Spirit today? This third question channels attention on how we have been in relationship with God, however we understand God. People from most every spiritual tradition long to encounter the Holy One, receive support and consolation, wisdom and understanding. Unfortunately, we often miss our opportunities.

In *Meditation from the Heart of Judaism*, Rabbi Rami Shapiro tells this story:

> A Hasid bust into the study of Reb Yerachmiel be Yisrael. "Rebbe," he said breathlessly, "what is the way to God?"

> The rebbe looked up from his studies and answered, "There is no way to God, for God is not other than here and now."

"Then, Rebbe, tell me the essence of God."

"There is no essence of God, for God is all and nothing."

"Then, Rebbe, tell me the secret that I might know that God is all."

"My friend," Reb Yerachmiel sighed, "there is no way, there is no essence, there is no secret. The truth you seek is not hidden from you. You are hiding from it."

The Spirit and the truth about our spirit is not hidden from us, we hide from them. Writing our response to the three questions brings us out of hiding from them and most specifically can open our eyes to the presence of God who is always present.

Recall the story of Moses' encounter with the Holy One who appeared in the burning bush. Under the direction of the Holy One, he was to lead the people out of slavery. Moses kept pointing out his own limitations as a leader, and God kept reassuring him. At one point, Moses tells God in effect, "I need to be able to tell the people your name, or they won't believe me." In reply, the answer came, "You shall say to the Israelites, 'I AM has sent me to you.'" Notice that the sacred name is not "I'm going to be" or "I was" but "I AM." This points to one aspect of the essence of the Holy: constant presence among and inside us. Every day, every moment.

Many millennia later, Henry David Thoreau, the transcendentalist, understood God in much the same way: "God himself culminates in the present moment, and will never be more divine in the lapse of all the ages. And we are enabled to apprehend at all what is sublime and noble only by the perpetual instilling and drenching of the reality that surrounds us." The reality around us is drenched and instilled with the sacred presence. We only need to listen and see just as Thoreau did when writing these words in his journal.

> "Why should I wish to see **God** better than **this day?** I see something of God **each hour** of the twenty-four, and each moment then."
>
> *Walt Whitman*

Writing our reflections on question 3 about our experience of the Spirit in our day reminds us of the divine Presence. In *The Irrational Season*, book 3 of *The Crosswicks Journal*, Madeleine L'Engle made this entry: "Easter: . . . A graduate student wrote to ask if my Christianity affects my novels, and I replied that

"The world is charged with the **grandeur of God.** It will flame out, like shining from shook foil; It gathers to a greatness, like the ooze of oil."

Gerard Manley Hopkins

it is the other way around. My writing affects my Christianity. In a way one might say that my stories keep converting me back to Christianity, from which I am constantly tempted to stray because the circle of blessing seems frayed and close to breaking, and my faith is so frail and flawed that I fall away over and over again from my God. There are times when I feel that he has withdrawn from me, and I have often given him cause; but Easter is always the answer to My God, my God, why hast thou forsaken me!" L'Engle's entry for Easter draws her back to the blessed reassurance of the Sacred Presence. Daily reflections on the presence of the Divine aids in the constant process of our "converting" back to a life filled with the Spirit of truth, a life lived with integrity, a life in harmony.

Write.

For daily journal writing, even if you begin with listing or flow writing, move into these three fundamental questions:

1. Have my actions and decisions today aligned with my beliefs?

2. How have I loved today?

3. How did I sense the presence of God or my Higher Power or Allah or The Holy One or the Ground of Being during the day? /OR/ What did I hear from the Spirit today?

chapter**six**

Looking**Back**

"**No man** can know where **he is going** unless he knows **exactly** where he has been and exactly how he arrived **at his present place.**"

Maya Angelou

Tell Me a Story

■ ■ ■ ■ ■ ■ ■ ■ ■ ■ ■ ■ ■

In a town in Eastern Europe lived a great rabbi, whose wisdom and leadership inspired a devout congregation. Whenever disaster threatened the community, he would go into the forest, light a fire, and say prayers that the community would be saved from disaster. And, they were.

When the renowned rabbi passed away, his successor tried to follow his example. So, when persecution hovered over the community, he would light a fire and say the prayers. "Master of the Universe, I do not know the place in the forest, but I have lighted the fire and offered the prayers." Once again, the community was saved from destruction.

When disaster threatened, his successor as rabbi would pray, "I do not know the place in the forest or how to light the fire, but I will say the prayers." And disaster swept away from the community.

Finally, the third successor to the great rabbi was confronted with leading the community when trouble came again. Lifting his eyes to the Holy One, he admitted, "I do not know the place in the forest or how to light the fire. I don't even know the prayers. All I can do is tell the story and that will have to do." And it did. Once again the community was saved from destruction.

Telling a story does save people from oblivion. Telling the story has always had the power to raise up and inform, inspire, and offer hope and perspective. That is the reason that every spiritual tradition has stories at the heart of their living tradition. The stories explain the values of the community and how God—whether named Allah, Brahman, or Adonai—has acted to save the people time and time again. Telling the story reminds people of who they are and what they stand for.

During the Easter Vigil celebrations, Christians hear the stories of God's actions in the life of the community: Creation, Exodus, and the Resurrection. Indeed, the whole Bible read by Christians—from the Creation story to the book of Revelations at the end—is one great story of how God has consistently entered into the human story to save women and men from destruction.

During the eight days of Passover, Jews listen to the story of the Exodus from bondage in Egypt. The high point is the Seder meal that includes recitation of the *Haggadah*, the central events of liberation as recounted in Exodus.

Muslims all over the world recount events from the life of the prophet Muhammad to remind themselves of the revelations of Allah. They tell the story of the Night of Power and Excellence, when Muhammad first heard Gabriel tell him: "Recite! Your Lord is the Most Beautiful One, who by the pen taught man what he did not know!" They are inspired by the story of Muhammad's *Hijra* or "emigration" and his Ascension to Heaven, when he was miraculously transported from Mecca to Jerusalem and then ascended with the archangel Gabriel through the seven heavens.

Families all have their stories that are told Thanksgiving after Thanksgiving. And organizations have stories too. Human beings tell stories so that they do not forget where they come from, who they are, and what they are called to be. Stories still save communities from disintegration, from oblivion.

Individual human beings have the same drive as communities to understand the past by telling its stories. Harriet A. Jacobs wrote her memoir *Incidents in the Life of a Slave Girl, Written by Herself* to let people know about the grinding oppression of slavery. She also reveals her courage, hopefulness, and wisdom. By telling her story, she unfolded it for herself and offers generations to come testament to the true nature of enslavement and to the dignity of the human spirit. The journal she kept and the memoir she wrote allow her the space for total honesty:

> There is a great difference between Christianity and religion at the south. If a man goes to the communion table, and pays money into the treasury of the church, no matter if it be the price of blood, he is called religious. If a pastor has offspring by a woman not his wife, the church dismisses him, if she is a white woman; but if she is colored, it does not hinder his continuing to be their good shepherd.

> When I was told that Dr. Flint had joined the Episcopal church, I was much surprised. I supposed that religion had a purifying effect on the character of men; but the worst persecutions

I endured from him were after he was a communicant.

[Flint told her she should join.] Rejoined I. "If I could be allowed to live like a Christian, I should be glad."

. . . "What right have you, who are my negro, to talk to me about what you would like, and what you wouldn't like? I am your master, and you shall obey men."

No wonder the slaves sing, —

"Ole Satan's church is here below;

Up to God's free church I hope to go."

This desire to recall and recount the past is inherent in human beings. People desire to remember and to be remembered.

Writers of journals and diaries, memoirs and autobiographies desire to remember and be remembered, too. In her book *Remembered Rapture*, Bell Hooks summarizes the impulse to look into the past to understand it: "The longing to tell one's story and the process of telling is symbolically a gesture of longing to recover the past in such a way that one experiences both a sense of reunion and a sense of release. It was the longing for release that compelled the writing but concurrently it was the joy of reunion that enabled me to see that the act of writing one's autobiography is a way to find again that aspect of the self and experience that may no longer be an actual part of one's life but is a living memory shaping and informing the present." Indeed, all that has gone before in life does give shape to the life lived now. To understand the present, people have always looked to the past.

When we think about what makes us who we are, particular events, relationships, meetings, and conversations come to mind spontaneously. Ira Progoff referred to these as "steppingstones." Former UN General Secretary Dag Hammarskjöld called them "markings," which became the title of his journal-memoir. Steppingstones may be painful or joyful, dramatic or quiet. Whatever the case, when we think of those points along our journey that made us who we are, our "markings" come immediately to mind.

To begin telling the story of the past, journal keepers can simply make lists of their markings—starting anywhere or writing them in five- or ten-year increments. Some diarists put "I remember" on a blank page and finish the sentence with phrases that will trigger memories of larger events. Other memoir writers do storylines. Using large sheets of poster board or butcher paper, crayons, pens, pencil, anything they wish, they chart out a story line for their life: the main events, decisions, and relationships of their life, the highs and lows, the key things that have led them to this moment and helped form their character.

Steppingstones or story lines can map out a life from birth through the present, or they can focus on one time-period's markings or one theme or topic. For example, if someone wanted to understand an important relationship better, she or he could trace the markings—the key moments—in that relationship: how it started, what happened next, other key events and conversations—all the way to the present. In effect, they would be outlining the story of the relationship. Markings or story lines can be done for failures and successes at school, work, or personal goals; romantic relationships; career; body events; projects; family, and so on.

These markings and storylines provide an overview of a person's general story or a facet of their overall story that can be explored more deeply. Markings often expose certain themes in our life that we may not have realized ran through it. That realization can send us in search of more understanding by doing the steppingstones or storyline of a particular theme: how it developed. Looking back in one of these ways opens up the story of our life to greater wisdom and understanding.

> "A journal-keeper is really the natural historian of his own life. But many of the **great journals** are marked by a dogged absence of self-consciousness, a willingness to **suspend judgment** of the journal itself."
>
> *Verlyn Klinkenborg*

Write!

To list these steppingstones it is best to begin with a period of relaxation, deep breathing, stretching, and quiet. Next, without writing yet, let your memory ponder, "What are my markings?" Then note whatever images, ideas, or events come to mind.

After a period of quiet remembering, simply list in phrases the markings that came to mind. Some people find it helpful to list the steppingstones in different age increments. But this is not really necessary. The important thing is to write the list quickly and spontaneously, without censoring or quibbling inside about the importance of an event.

To aid in memory of key events, some journal writers look through collected photos from their lives and scrapbooks that they have kept. This can be quite effective in jogging memory.

Our Myth

Each person is largely the product of all that has happened in her or his life up to the present. It is important to ask, "Where am I?" Even so, if people are to understand the texture of their lives, looking back proves indispensably instructive. Chapter 2 offered this adage:

Plant an act; reap a habit.

Plant a habit; reap a virtue or vice.

Plant a virtue or vice; reap a character.

Plant a character; reap a destiny.

Diarists can arrive at a clearer understanding of their destiny if they trace back through their stories to examine the acts that grew into habits and developed into their virtues and vices.

Hindus and Buddhists use the word *karma,* the moral law of cause and

"In the safety of the journal's pages, we can examine what lies beneath our 'apparent' emotions, trace the past and present associations that interweave in our emotional lives, and get closer to the real heart of the matter."

Marlene A. Schiwy

effect, to describe destiny. *Karma* means that every action has some effect that is either morally good or morally evil. In the biblical tradition, people are taught that they reap what they sow. In either case, a person's *karma* or destiny is shaped by each decision and the resulting actions and consequences. So, to thoroughly understand where I am, I need to understand where I've been and what I've done—the habits, vices/virtues, and character formed.

In effect, these formative stories are a person's individual *myth.* In his conversations with mythologist Joseph Campbell, Bill Moyers described myth this way: "Myths are stories of our search through the ages for truth, for meaning, for significance. We all need to tell our story and to understand our story." Campbell added a slight twist to Moyers' description. He responded: "I think that what we're seeking is an experience of being alive. . . . Myths are clues to the spiritual potentialities of the human life." In other words, a person's *myth* is the story of their experiences of being alive. The important stories that people remember, hold on to, and retell form their own myth: the story of their experience of what it means for them to be really alive.

Just as members of all religious traditions recount their myths century after century in order to declare their identity, share essential truths and values, and to quite literally stay alive, so individuals do the same. One need only think of women and men who lived through any war.

They often hold onto their war stories as expressions of the most intense and meaningful times of their lives. Whether joyous times or tragic times, a person's stories offer listeners or readers or the writer him or herself a glimpse into the person's experience of really living: their myth.

The beauty of sharing stories is that people realize that they are not alone. Others have been through what they have been through and survived. Even if we do not share our myth, the act of writing it can be healing because while looking back, we gain a richer appreciation of our power and resources. In *No More Words: A Journal of My Mother, Anne Morrow Lindbergh*, Reeve Lindbergh told the following story:

> When I lost my first son just before his second birthday, she who had also lost her first son [who was killed by a kidnapper] knew what to say, and she was one of the few people I was willing to listen to. She told me the truth first. . . . "This horror will fade, I can promise you that. The horror fades. The sadness, though, is different. The sadness remains. . . ."
>
> That, too, was correct. The horror faded. I left it behind me in that terrible winter, but the sadness remained. Gradually, over the years, it became a member of my family, like our old dog sleeping in the corners. . . .

"Writing has been the constancy through which I have reinvented myself after every uprooting."

Mary Catherine Bateson

At the time of my son's death, when I asked my mother what would happen to me as the mother of the child, how that part of me would continue, she said, "It doesn't. You die, that's all. That part of you dies with him. And then, amazingly, you are reborn. . . ."

I was reborn into a whole different life with my second.

Such stories as those of Reeve and Anne Morrow Lindbergh strengthened them and enlighten readers today because, as Joseph Campbell declared, "They're stories about the wisdom of life."

Writing about the past—the personal myth—with all its joys and sorrows helps the writer discover the wisdom and spirit that can sustain them whatever the future brings. *Karma* is not fate. *Karma* or destiny can be changed by being conscious of the wisdom of the past and by making decisions and planting acts that lead toward life.

Write!

Writer Patricia Hampl declares, "We only store in memory images of value." The list of "markings" in the first Write! exercise of this chapter provides some "images of value." To begin writing your own personal myth, take these "images of value" and describe the who, what, when, where, how, and often, why of the event:

1. Who was involved?

2. What happened?

3. When did it happen?

4. Where did it take place?

5. How did the event transpire and how were people affected?

6. Why did this happen?

A personal myth emerges from such stories. When writing these stories, John Kotre's words from *White Gloves: How We Create Ourselves Through Memory* can provide some encouragement and direction:

"All men should **strive to learn** before they die what they are running from, and to, **and why.**"

James Thurber

As a maker of myth, the self leaves its handiwork everywhere in memory. With the passing of time, the good guys in our lives get a little better and the bad guys a little worse. The speeds get faster, the fish gets bigger, the Depression gets tougher. . . . All distortions of memory, all the reconstructions, all the phantom imlants—so out of place on a witness stand—appear in a different light when seen as narrative embellishments. . . . Such alterations are not the edicts of a dictator, but the signs of a mythmaker. They tell us who it is that's doing the remembering.

In other words, memory will always massage the facts. That's the nature of storytelling. Myths are true, even if they are not literally factual.

Stories Within Stories: The Genogram

Every story from a person's past leads to other stories. Indeed, every story has been touched by untold numbers of other stories. Certain attitudes about music and hard work were passed on to me by my German-emigrant grandparents. My religious background has a story, too. My mother's father was raised Catholic, but seldom went to church. Nevertheless, every Sunday, he had my Lutheran grandmother march all eight kids off to St. Mary's Catholic Church. My dad's mother came from a long line of staunch German Catholics. On the other hand, my unchurched, great grandfather Koch told my grandfather as a boy growing up in Clinton, Louisiana, that he should choose a religion because it was important for getting along here in America. So my grandfather selected Catholicism, two great-uncles joined the Presbyterians, and one the Lutherans.

Every person can trace certain beliefs, practices, rituals, and familial sayings back to someone else. Each of these beliefs and practices has effects in shaping a person's character, physique, medical history, and so on. One way of discovering the stories behind the story is to construct a genogram. Peter Gilmour, in *The Wisdom of Memoir*, describes genograms this way: "The genogram [assists] people in establishing and interpreting their place within their intergenerational families of origin. . . . The physical, intellectual, and spiritual dimensions of identity are revealed in the process and product . . . and tracing one's lineage . . . can help a person understand determinants of identity and provide a route to freedom."

Genealogy: Constructing a genogram begins by doing a genealogical chart back as many generations as possible. Genealogists suggest many different formats, but for most people a simple sketching can serve nicely. On a large piece of paper they write their name at the bottom in a box, then draw a line up to their parents' names on a line above on which are listed the names of all their aunts and uncles. Above the parents are listed the names of grandparents with their siblings—the great aunts and uncles; above that are listed great-grandparents and anyone from that generation whose names can be remembered. In short, the genealogy becomes an illustration of the family tree.

Bloodlines: Memoir writers or journal writers looking to the past often find a rich source of understanding by tracing the ethnic, national, and cultural origins of their ancestors. They can do this by jotting down a sentence or two about each grandparent, aunt, uncle, cousin, or parent that describes how each one reflects their ethnic, national, or cultural heritage. Then, they ask this question: "How has my heritage influenced me?" So, for example, "How has my German, Catholic, Memphis/New Orleans of the 1950s heritage influenced me?" After all, each person is influenced by her or his ethnic, national, or cultural ancestry, so answering the question leads the writer to look for stories or examples of how their heritage has shaped them in the present. Listing some of these influences and the stories opens up whole new territories for exploration.

Thoughtlines: Each person has also been touched and formed by an ancestry of key ideas or concepts that they have been taught. Some of these ideas are eternal truths (for example, love as a key moral principle) and others can be warped (for instance, slavery is a right). But whether people consider themselves intellectuals or not, all have a storehouse of ideas that they depend on, and they learned these ideas somewhere. Again, many people find tracing these thoughtlines back to their sources is a helpful way to understand themselves more fully.

> **"All my stories have been written with material that was gathered—no, God save us! not gathered but absorbed— before I was fifteen years old."**
>
> *Willa Cather*

The process is simple. They list some ideas or principles that they hold most dear. If this is hard to do, sometimes people list their heroes—people who symbolize key principles for them. Then, after each idea or principle—or thoughtline—they try to answer these questions: How did this idea enter my life? Who was most influential in teaching me this idea or principle? How has this idea guided my actions or how did I fight this principle and live to regret it? What have been the consequences of making this idea or principle part of my life?

Constructing a simple genealogy and writing bloodlines and thoughtlines move writers in the direction of greater comprehension of the richness of their stories. In an autobiographical sketch, poet Denise Levertov reflects this: "'Who are you? And how did you become what you are?' are questions which, when I try to answer them honestly, increase my awareness of how strong, in my case (where in others place and community often play a dominant part), were inherited tendencies and the influence of the cultural milieu—unsupported by a community—of my own family. My father's Hasidic ancestry, his being steeped in Jewish and Christian scholarship and mysticism, his fervor and eloquence as a preacher, were factors built into my cells. . . . My mother's Welsh intensity and lyric feeling for Nature were not just the air I breathed but, surely, were in the body I breathed with." All people are more than simply what they have done since birth. They are formed and shaped by the larger story out of which they have sprung. It must be accounted for.

Write!

Following the directions above, construct a genealogy of your ancestry. Then, using the other directions, compose bloodlines and thoughtlines. To move deeper into your heritage, write a story or stories based on a cultural or ethnic influence or thoughtline that has been particularly important in forming you into the person you are. Such storytelling further enhances the adventure of looking into the past.

The Spirit's Story

Every person's spiritual development has its story, too. In *An American Childhood*, Annie Dillard describes a key moment in her spiritual journey. Sitting in the balcony of her church, she experienced the Spirit's quiet voice:

> In the crowded nave, men and women were also concentrating, it seemed. Were they perhaps pretending to pray? All heads were bent; no one moved. . . .

> For I knew these people, didn't I? . . . I knew what they loved: their families, their houses, their country clubs, hard work, the people they knew best, and summer parties with old friends full of laughter. . . .

> Nevertheless a young father below me propped his bowed head on two fists stacked on a raised knee. . . . No one moved. The organist hushed. All the men's heads were bent—black, white, red, yellow, and brown. The men sat absolutely still. Almost all the women's heads were bent down, too, and some few tilted back. . . .

I was alert enough now to feel, despite myself, some faint, thin stream of spirit braiding forward from the pews. Its flawed and fragile rivulets pooled far beyond me at the altar. I felt, or saw, its frail strands rise to the wide tower ceiling, and mass in the gold mosaic's dome.

This was an important moment in Dillard's spiritual development, which she goes on to explore in the rest of her memoir.

Most people have these key moments when they draw toward a particular religious practice or turn their back on a church, when they have sudden experiences of the Divine or long periods of

"It's not so much the imperfect words on these faint blue lines, as the feeling, time and again, of **returning to a place** from which one can continue to spin one and the same thread, where one can gradually **create a continuum,** a continuum which is really one's life."

Etty Hillesum

doubt, fear, and sense of abandonment. Some of the great religious conversion stories have become perennial bestsellers: Augustine's *Confessions,* Julian of Norwich's *Showings,* Thomas Merton's *Seven Storey Mountain* are only three. And these personal stories of spirit are still being written by authors churched and unchurched. Just one of the better known contemporary spiritual memoirs is Kathleen Norris's *Dakota: A Spiritual Geography.* Norris declares early on: "More than any other place I lived as a child or young adult . . . this is my spiritual geography, the place where I've wrestled my story out of the circumstances of the landscape and geography." Writers of memoir—maybe especially spiritual memoir—are always "wrestling" their stories out of their experience.

Why people write of their spiritual journey may be explained by Jack Kornfield when he says: "Our hearts shine in the same way as the fireflies, with the same light as the sun and the moon. Within us is a secret longing to remember this light, to step out of time, to feel our true place in this dancing world. It's where we began and where we return." Telling the spiritual story invites writers back into the light where they find their true place in the world. So they tell their stories of spirit.

As with bloodlines and thoughtlines though, our spirituality has been formed by countless influences: our parents, friends, experience of nature and transcendence, and so on. In looking at the spiritual journey, the full richness of the journey can only be understood when all of these influences are taken into account. Jesus of the Gospels acknowledges the host of ancestors in his spiritual story, recorded in the genealogy of the opening chapter of the Gospel according to Matthew (cf. 1: 1–17). Jesus was a Jew, rooted in the whole story of Abraham, Moses, David, and the prophets. Tibetan Buddhists trace their spiritual story back through generations of lamas, and ultimately to Gautama Buddha. Shia Muslims are guided by imams living and dead, but all go back through Ali to the Prophet Muhammad. All spiritual stories need to look back at those who have gone before.

By looking back at all the influences, a spiritual seeker starts making the kind of important connections that writer

"I believe that if one person gains spiritually the whole world gains, and if one person falls, the world falls to that extent."

Mohandas Gandhi

"The next thing most like **living one's life** over again seems to be a recollection of that life, and to make that recollection as durable as possible by putting it **down in writing."**

Benjamin Franklin

Eudora Welty describes: "Writing is one way of discovering sequence in experience. . . . Connections slowly emerge. Like distant landmarks you are approaching, cause and effect begin to align themselves. . . . Experiences . . . connect and are identified as a larger shape." Finding this "larger shape" and the light are the treasures found in looking back at the spiritual geography.

Write!

Every aspect of our spirituality has its story, a spiritual story line. Here is a process of tracing the spiritual story. Start by working chronologically, perhaps in ten-year increments, listing phrases that capture important moments in your spiritual-religious story. These questions may help trigger memories:

1. What were dominant images of God in each time segment? Or, did you have an image?
2. What were the most meaningful spiritual experiences, not necessarily in a church, mosque, or synagogue?
3. What were some sacred places for you?
4. What were the most meaningful spiritual experiences in a place of religious worship?
5. Who were some people who strongly influenced your spiritual values? Try to list particular times with each one that stands out as important.
6. What were your parents and other family members' religious beliefs that influenced you?
7. Did any social or historical events influence how you regard religion and spirituality?
8. Have any particular religious or spiritual rituals been important?
   Pick one core moment on your spiritual journey and write the story of that moment.

chapterseven

Staying in Dialogue

"Every afternoon I discipline myself to record **my feelings** and insights in my journal.

I am compelled to bring them to consciousness.

I write and I write, trying to find meaning in my suffering. **My journal is my lifeline.**"

Mary Hamilton

The Dynamics of Dialogue

Dialogues are always going on inside us. Ideas flow back and forth as a person contemplates buying the blue bedspread or the green one. While furious with a supervisor, a salesperson holds an imagined conversation during which she lambastes the jerk, saying all the biting, clever things she would never say out loud for fear of being fired. A job candidate role-plays the interview with a prospective employer, taking both sides of the conversation. These internal dialogues happen all the time, and they can serve us well as we work through issues—even though sometimes we would like to shut them off.

Every person we have met, event that we have been a part of, and our body-story all have a place inside us. They become part of who we are. After my friend and colleague Margarette died of cancer, sometimes I would find myself remembering her. She was a marvelous teacher, from whom I learned invaluable lessons. I would wonder what she would do when faced with a particularly difficult student. And I would vividly remember the only time I heard her express complete frustration with one of her students. Walking by her office one day, I saw her sitting at her desk, shaking her head. All she said was, "That young man has so little sense that his brain rattles around in his head like a bee-bee in a boxcar." So when I felt myself wondering what to do, I would carry on a dialogue with Margarette, always emerging more calm and confident. At the time I didn't fully realize what I was doing. When I began journaling, I began to comprehend the value of these dialogues and started writing them down.

Inside every person are many relationships—some with their demons and others with their angels. Whether they like to admit it or not, they carry on these inner dialogues. The journal writer turns these inner dialogues into a source of integration and understanding. As Christina Baldwin remarks, "Dialogue writing releases insight from two angles rather than one. . . . Dialogue requires that you trust yourself to play both roles, to write in multiple voices."

In *The Good Times*, Russell Baker provides a good example of a telling dialogue. It's a patchwork of what his mother always said to him filled with phrases that are part of his consciousness. His mother still lives within him, and he can still talk with her because she *is* there in his memory:

> My mother, dead now to this world but still roaming free in my mind, wakes me some mornings before daybreak. "If there's one thing I can't stand, it's a quitter." I have heard her say that all my life. Now, lying in bed, coming awake in the dark, I feel the fury of her energy fighting

the good-for-nothing idler within me who wants to go back to sleep instead of tackling the brave new day.

Silently I protest: I am not a child anymore. I have made something of myself. I am entitled to sleep late.

"Russell, you've got no more gumption than a bump on a log. Don't you want to amount to something?"

She has hounded me with these same battle cries since I was a boy in short pants back in the Depression.

"Amount to something!"

"Make something of yourself!"

"Don't be a quitter!"

On bad mornings, in the darkness, suspended between dreams and daybreak, with my mother racketing around in my head, I feel crushed by failure.

Sometimes these inner dialogues are painful and at others joyous, but in either case they are revealing. Baker, a successful writer, still deals with the inner voice of his long dead mother. Writing may be the only way of exorcising the harsh messages and recovering balance.

Always though, writing key conversations can enlighten writers about central moments in their story. It's not so important that they are a verbatim account. That is generally impossible and totally unnecessary. What is important is that writers play both roles: theirs and the other person's or the event's. Writing dialogue has proven to be a marvelous way to understand people, the body-self, and events in deeper, often surprising ways.

Writing the dialogues has another benefit. While writing a dialogue the writer has an opportunity to change the conversation, to try new words and responses, and to reframe the relationship. Christian Baldwin remarks, "One of the greatest powers of journal writing is that over time it helps us notice, influence, and change the conversation the mind is having with itself." In his talk as part of the Sacred Stories series for the Trinity Institute, Frederick Buechner offers a dramatic example of this in a dialogue he wrote with his long-dead father.

His father had taken his own life when Buechner was a boy. The family never, ever talked about it. Indeed, they kept their feelings and reactions locked tight within the family and within themselves. For decades Buechner, the renowned novelist, minister, and speaker, kept trying to come to grips with this defining moment, this marking, in his life. Finally, a therapist suggested that Buechner—then in his fifties—write a dialogue with his father, but using his left hand (he writes with his right hand), the idea being that he would only write what was absolutely at the heart of the matter. Here is part of the dialogue that Buechner wrote:

Child: Were you very sad? Were you scared, Daddy? Did you know what you were going to do?

Father: I had to do it. Things were so bad. There wasn't any other way out.

Child: Could I have stopped you, Daddy, if I told you I loved you? If I told you I needed you?

Father: No. Nobody could. I was lost so badly.

Child: Is this really you I'm talking to? I can't see your face. I've forgotten your face, your smell.

Father: I remember you. I was proud of you. I wanted you to like me.

Child: I've been so worried. I've been so scared ever since.

Father: Don't be. There's nothing to worry about. That's the secret I never knew. I know it now.

Child: What do you know, Daddy, my dearest Dad?

Father: I know plenty, and it's all good. I will see you again. Be happy for me. It's my birthday present to you. I loved you boys. I love you still.

Child: I love you. Good-bye for now.

Father: So long, Fritz. Everything's going to be all
right.

Buechner recounts this dialogue because it helped him
heal this ancient wound and allay his secret fears. As with
all journal writing, in writing the dialogue, he could now
reframe that terrible day long ago when his father sat on
the running board of his car and waited for the fumes to
kill him.

Was it really Buechner's father talking with him? Of
course. His father was inside him, just as the answers to his
questions were. By engaging in the conversation, he
rediscovered a truth that set him free from old, old fears.
This is often one of the great gifts of dialogue writing. Like
the suicide of Buechner's father, events and persons from
the past often invite further exploration. They lurk in our
memories and appear in our dreams until they are met and
understood. As in any relationship, especially one of
conflict, dialogue can often bring some peace.

Write!

Most journal writers encounter many unanswered questions and much unfinished business as they look back in their stories. They remember events that still impact their life, but wonder why. They recall relationships that ended badly and still bother their dreams. Whatever the case, in each life, there is usually some unfinished business or a broken relationship that could be met and profit from dialogue.

To begin the dialogues, make a list of important events and relationships noted as markings or steppingstones or simply go back and review those already recorded. By searching through the steppingstones, you can list those key events that have inner importance.

These events may not be as tragic or dramatic as the suicide of Buechner's father. The key criterion for selection is: As you read slowly through the markings of your life, does an event or relationship seem to invite more reflection or further memory? Progoff advises: "The main factor to consider is not whether there is a problem involved in the relationship [or event], but whether we feel that the relationship [or event] itself plays a role of inner importance in our life. . . . Our emotions give us criterion enough to judge their inner importance for our life." So, listing relationships and events of "inner importance" is the starting place for your dialogues.

Dialogues with People

We build relationships with many others. If they are important in some way, people then take up residence inside us. As time passes, a whole community of persons lives within us. Once when I was in serious conflict with a coworker, I would come home moaning and complaining, ranting and raving about this person. In effect, he took up residence in our house. I knew that I had to deal with the relationship when my wife asked me when he was going to start paying rent. Since we weren't talking face to face very successfully, I wrote many dialogues with him, trying to understand where he was coming from and how I was pushing his buttons. In the process, I had a clearer picture of what set me off and what I might do to help the situation. I can't say we ever totally ironed things out, but it helped me gain perspective.

> "Even one person can have a **sense of dialogue** within himself, if the **spirit of the dialogue is present.**"
>
> *David Bohm*

Written dialogues are ways of talking with people who embody some unexplored aspect of ourselves. The person we select for dialogue should be someone whose life and actions have an important bearing on our own life, as we perceive it. The technique can be used as a form of interior role-playing, in which we carry on a dialogue with someone with whom we are in conflict, in love, and so on, to put ourselves inside their shoes.

We have sharp memories of important bits of advice, key warnings, or dire admonitions. In carrying on dialogues that we write as explorations now, we do not need to fear that we won't remember what the other person would say. Zora Neale Hurston (1901–1960) grew up in an all-black Florida town. Her passion for education eventually took her to New York, where she learned the methods of ethnographers and folklorists, part of which was interviewing. When she wrote her own memoir, *Dust Tracks on a Road,* in her later years, she recalled the voices and advice that shaped her. While she did not use a dialogue form like Baker or Buechner, her readers and Hurston herself hear what her mother and father said and so gain a sense of what she replied:

Mama exhorted her children at every opportunity to "jump at de sun." We might not land on the sun, but at least we would get off the ground. Papa did not feel so hopeful. Let well enough alone. It did not do for Negroes to have too much spirit. He was always threatening to break mine or kill me in the attempt. My mother was always standing between us. She conceded that I was impudent and given to talking back, but she didn't want to "squinch my spirit" too much for fear that I would turn out to be a mealy-mouthed rag doll by the time I got grown. Papa always flew hot when Mama said that. I do not know whether he feared for my future, with the tendency I had to stand and give battle, or that he felt a personal reference in Mama's observation. He predicted dire things for me. The white folks were not going to stand for it. I was going to be hung before I got grown.

Writing about what her Mama and Papa said to her and to each other reveals a lot about Hurston's character and how it developed. This summary kind of dialogue was certainly a sample of the words that her parents used to mold who she became.

The dialogues between Baker and his mother, Buechner and his father, and Hurston and her parents helped them understand their relationships with these significant

"**A writer** is not so much someone who has something to say as he is someone **who has found a process** that will bring about **new things** he would not have thought of if he had not started to say them."

William Stafford

people. In effect, they were exercises in empathy. By taking both sides of the conversation, they chose to put themselves into the shoes of their parents to see themselves and life as their parents did. In her book *Changing the Bully that Rules the World*, Carol Bly adds that these dialogues are also exercises in "reversible thinking" that takes empathy a step further: "We are doing reversible thinking when we deliberately pretend not only that we are inside another person but also that that other person is looking back at and judging us." Assuming the role of the other person in the dialogue assists writers in more fully seeing themselves as others see them and understanding themselves in new ways.

And empathy is essential for living fully, living ethically. Compassion and love are impossible for persons who cannot put themselves into the shoes of someone else. Compassion and love are rooted in knowledge of the real needs and best good of the other. If their needs are not understood from their point of view, a person, even with the best of intentions, may end up doing only what she or he thinks is best and not what is truly the best for the other. Many well-meaning aid agencies have learned this the hard way. For instance, an international aid organization gave the Philippine government a huge grant to build low-cost housing for Manila's throngs of homeless people. Planners designed a simple concrete block, tin roofed house, complete with running water. With the grant, they could have built thousands of these decent houses. A high-ranking official looked at the plans, declared that she would not let anyone live in such shabby housing, and dictated that condominium style housing should be built. As a result, the poor people who would have been delighted with the simple houses remained homeless.

This same sort of thing happens in personal relationships. We are only one-half of the reality. Our truth may not be the truth of the other. Empathy takes us out of ourselves, so we see from both sides. Be warned though: Empathy and reversible thinking as exercised in the dialogues can take us out of our comfort zone. As Carol Bly notes: "As soon as one wakes up ethically, nothing is clean cut." However, everything becomes more lively and real.

There are many effective approaches to writing dialogues with people. Simply sitting down and beginning the conversation with a question and then writing the answer can lead into dialogue. Here are some steps that take writing dialogues with people into deeper water. Some of the preliminary steps can be skipped, but each step adds additional insight. What's most important is to engage in the dialogue.

1. Sit quietly and breathe deeply. This can help open your mind to dialogue writing. Now write the name of a person with whom you wish to dialogue. (Your steppingstones or markings provide a wealth of people from the past with whom to converse, or you may have someone from your daily journal with whom a conversation may be more pressing.) Spending some moments remembering encounters with the person and tapping into any resulting feelings prepare you for dialogue.

2. Writing a short description of the relationship in the present helps your recollection. You can do this even when the other person is deceased. After reading the description, any additions or clarifications can be written. Always note what you are feeling as you write the description.

3. List and look at the markings or key moments in the relationship and highlight defining points that have led to where the relationship is now. Indeed, any unfinished business can be a good subject with which to begin a dialogue. Buechner's dialogue with his father cleared up important unfinished business.

4. After a period of quiet, begin the dialogue. Many people start with a question that they need to ask. Others begin with a greeting and then enter the dialogue, letting the conversation flow back and forth until a natural ending point occurs. Dialogues can be written in "play" form like Buechner's, narrative form like Baker's, or more free form like Hurston's. What's essential is that each voice gets a chance to speak honestly, bluntly, and completely.

5. At the end of the dialogue, note your feelings. After reading through the dialogue, aloud if possible, note your reactions. Some writers find it helpful to ask if they need to take any action as a result of the dialogue.

Dialogues with Defining Moments

Not only do people become part of the fabric of a person's being, so do key events—those defining moments that change us. These moments may be dramatic or quiet, obvious or only understood long after. In any case, defining moments require a response from us, and that response has consequences on the shape of our life. In this sense, defining moments become part of every person's character and destiny.

One of Madeline L'Engle's defining moments came when she "first became aware of myself as self" at seven or eight years old. Years later she wrote of it in *A Circle of Quiet*, book 1 of *The Crosswicks Journal:*

"I can **become you** for a second and you can **become me** and this lifts us up."

Meryl Streep

One evening when I was looking out [her bedroom window] I saw a woman undressing by her open window. She took off her dress, stretched, stood there in her slip, not moving, not doing anything, just standing there, being.

And that was my moment of awareness . . . : that woman across the court who did not know me, and whom I did not know, was a person. She had thoughts of her own. She *was*. Our lives would never touch. . . . And yet it was she who revealed to me my first glimpse of personhood.

When I woke in the morning the wonder of that revelation was still with me. . . .

I got out of bed and stood in front of the mirror and for the first time looked at myself consciously. I, too, was real, standing there thin and gawky in a white nightgown. I did more than exist. I *was*.

That afternoon when I went to the park I looked at everybody I passed on the street, full of the wonder of their realness.

This seemingly small event became—literally—a defining moment for L'Engle. From then on she became a self and began to realize the uniqueness of everyone else around her. The event became part of her. Writing about the event—in some sense conversing with it—long after its occurrence opened the event to her understanding.

Every event in people's lives has some import, whether they comprehend the import or not. In the journal, a writer regularly asks "Where am I?", keeps a daily record of her or his life, periodically explores the past, but also can engage in dialogue with events so as to enrich her or his understanding of some moment in the flow of experience.

Dialogues may be written with any event, but certainly moments that have had what Progoff calls "inner importance" may yield the greatest fruit. How do we know an event of "inner importance"? A key might be that this event keeps coming into consciousness over the years at times unbidden and certainly when writing the markings of one's life. Defining moments are most often recognized only in hindsight. Understanding them becomes the work of the dialogue.

To dialogue with an event, the journal writer begins listing events spontaneously and freely. An obvious starting point to find defining moments is to examine the markings from the previous chapter. A defining moment is one after which our life was different in some way. Defining moments might be: a critical illness, the decision to quit the football team in ninth grade, winning a gold medal at the state speech contest, being arrested for DUI, making love for the first time, entering a business partnership, snubbing a person who later became famous, and so on. Besides these more obvious markings are events that are recalled periodically, that come as a surprise and cause us to ask, "Why am I thinking about that now?"

Once a list of defining moments has emerged on the page, the next step is to select one of them that somehow invites exploration. The event can then be described: who, what, when, where, why, and how? Detail is not essential at this point; the bare facts will trigger memory.

As with the dialogue with people, tracing the key moments leading up to and away from the event—listing the markings of the event—will lead to a fuller sense of what happened. For example, if a main event was taking a BA with honors, a marking might be the person's parents reading to them when they were little, their first library card, or something similar.

Once the story of the defining moment has been laid out and pondered, a person is ready to enter the dialogue. A question may be posed at the beginning, then the event answers, and the dialogue continues. So, for instance, the writer might ask:

> Writer: When I look at my life up until now, the best moment was walking across that stage and getting my degree. I have three great kids and a good marriage, so why is that still so important to me?

> Honors: Wasn't that the first time you really felt like you had done something your parents couldn't?

And so on. The writer and the honors award try to come to some understanding, to answer a question that has nagged the writer for years.

Conversing with defining moments may at first seem strange. After all, how does one talk to an event? It's important to remember that every event is part of us. In effect, dialoguing with an event is actually an internal conversation with that part of us that the event has become. If the event is going to be integrated into who we are and become a source of strength and character, dialoguing with it becomes essential.

"Memory **believes** before knowing **remembers.**"

William Faulkner

Write!

Using the process of the dialogue with defining moments, invite yourself to explore one of the key moments in your life by writing a conversation with it.

Conversing with Our Body-Self

Reports about the rising percentage of obese people regularly make the news. Advertisements for diet plans fill the airwaves, along with come-ons about super-sized hamburgers and fries. Supplements to help us bulk up are hawked right after ads for products that will shrink our wrinkles. This maelstrom of conflicting messages about our bodies leaves people confused, frustrated, and sometimes numb.

Many people grow disconnected to a sense of their body-self until an illness strikes. Then they pay attention. Instead of appreciating, nurturing, and being aware of our body-self, most people have been taught to simply use the body and forget about it. But health and wholeness begin with awareness and attentiveness. Tibetan monk Pema Chodron remarked: "It's also helpful to realize that this very body that we have, that's stirring right here right now . . . with its aches and its pleasures . . . is exactly what we need to be full human, full awake, fully alive." Indeed, human beings are embodied spirits. The human body expresses love, service, wisdom, hope, and creativity.

And, the body-self has its own wisdom to offer. Even so, with our heads full of the welter of competing information and misinformation, we may have forgotten how to listen. Every ache and pain is a message, as is each feeling of exhilaration and burst of energy. As Marion Woodman says, "When the body is finally listened to it becomes eloquent. It's like changing a fiddle into a Stradivarius." Listening to the body-self can become a habit of self-care that leads to health and joy in living.

> "We must learn to **dip ourselves in the universe** at our gates, and know it, not from without by comprehension, but **from within.**"
>
> *Evelyn Underhill*

In a book I wrote with Joyce, my wife, *God Knows You'd Like a New Body: 12 Ways to Befriend the One You've Got*, we encouraged readers to "befriend" their bodies. We chose this term because our research and experience showed that many people did not view their bodies as friends—if they thought about their bodies at all. We wanted them to befriend their bodies for two reasons: (1) We almost always act in the best interests of our friends; and (2) Since many of us have become alienated or dissociated from our bodies, we need to become acquainted once again.

How do people become friends? In many cases their relationship begins with a conversation. Over the space of time, the friendship grows through many conversations. So, journal writers can befriend their body-selves by initiating conversations with their body-selves. As with dialoguing with events, it may seem strange at first, but as the conversations progress, friendship can grow. Almost every weight loss program requires a food log to keep track of caloric and fiber intake. Writing dialogues with the body takes this practice a large step further. Not only do these conversations help us stay physically healthy, they also can help us make a new friend out of someone we may have ignored far too long.

Write!

Certainly, like dialogues with persons or events, we can just start the conversation with our body-self with a question or statement, but some groundwork enriches the conversation. Much like when we first meet someone we find out about where they're from, what they do, and so on, dialogues with our body-self can begin by becoming reacquainted.

1. So, a good place to begin is by writing a spontaneous life history of your body. First, try to recall past experiences that relate to any aspect of your physical life, and then record them briefly—a word or phrase: "I broke my thumb in the eighth grade." "I started weight-lifting five years ago." List as many body markings as you can, attempting to recall some for each period of your life: infancy, childhood, adolescence, and so on.

2. After listing your body markings, read through your memories; notice any themes or images that come to mind. These themes and your feelings should be noted.

3. Next, write a brief, *non-judgmental* description of your attitudes about and relationship with your body as it is now, answering the question: "Where am I about my body-self now?"

4. Then, sit in silence and just ponder what you have written—the defining moments of your body's story and how you feel right now, letting any feelings, questions, or concerns come to consciousness.

5. When you feel ready to dialogue with our body-self—perhaps because a question keeps arising or a concern develops—simply start writing the dialogue, beginning with your question. Let the body-self respond, respecting the fact that your body-self has its own wisdom to offer. People coping with cancer or some other life-threatening illness have written many memoirs that are really dialogues with the body-self. All we are doing in these dialogues is conversing before a health crisis forces us to pay attention to our body-self.

6. At some natural stopping place, simply close the conversation, read the dialogue, note any surprises or revelations, and perhaps give thanks for the remarkable body-self that you are: "We are the Creator's work of art, created for the good works which God has already designated to make up our way of life" (Paul to the Ephesians).

You may continue further dialogs with images of your body-self, your diet, certain body parts, and body experiences. If you want to deepen your connections with your body-self keeping a daily log about your body, recording objectively your body reality day by day, can lead to more conversations and awareness: befriending.

exploring a great spiritual practice

chaptereight

Encountering the Holy

"**The Spirit in truth is all.** Those who know the Spirit dwelling in the **secret place of the heart** cut the bonds of ignorance even in this human life."

The Upanishads

Praying Our Experiences

One useful definition of prayer is "being aware of the Holy and responding to that awareness." So prayer begins by paying attention to signs of the Sacred and then responding in some way, whether that response is singing a song, reciting a prayer, or simply being silently attentive. God, our Higher Power, the Holy One, Allah— whatever name is used—is most typically met in a person's day to day life: through their experiences.

From time immemorial, people have met God in *nature*. Moses met God in the burning bush. The prophet Elijah went to the mountain to meet God, who was going to "pass by": "There was a great wind, but the Holy One was not in the wind. After the wind was an earthquake, but again, God was not in the earthquake. Then fire on the mountain, but the Creator of the universe was not there either. After the fire, at last, the Holy One came in a soft murmuring sound." Muhammad received his revelations on a mountain. The Buddha became enlightened as he sat under the fig tree. Written down, these encounters take their place in the world's sacred literature.

In all ages, people have encountered reflections of the Divine in other *people* who have been made in "the image of God." Surgeon Richard Selzer wrote in his journal about one of his encounters with the Holy One:

I stand by the bed where the young woman lies. . . . A tiny twig of the facial nerve, one of the muscles of her mouth, has been severed. . . . To remove the tumor in her cheek, I had cut this little nerve. Her young husband was in the room. He stands on the opposite side of the bed, and together they seem to be in a world all their own in the evening lamplight. . . .

Who are they? I ask myself. . . . "Will my mouth always be like this?" she asks. "Yes," I say, "it will. It is because the nerve was cut." She nods and is silent. But the young man smiles. "I like it," he says. "It's kind of cute."

All at once I know who he is. I understand, and I lower my gaze. One is not bold in an encounter with the divine. Unmindful, he bends to kiss her crooked mouth, and I am so close I can see how he twists his own lips to accommodate to hers . . . to show that their kiss still works.

Such love in people mirrors the Creator's love. Such moments of love form the "bands of love" (Hosea 11:4) with which God invites humanity into the divine embrace.

In short, people of all faiths and walks of life have encountered God in their *experiences*. When we pay attention to these experiences, note them, and listen to them, we are praying. In his book *Praying Our Experiences*, Joseph Schmidt remarks: "Praying our experiences is the practice of reflecting on and entering honestly into our everyday experiences in order to become aware of God's word in them and to offer ourselves through them to God. We are getting in touch with who we are as people who have had personal experiences and are offering our whole self to God through reflection on the events in our life." This praying of our experiences is perhaps the most basic form of prayer and meditation and is often done by writing in a journal.

Recall that in chapter 2 writing the journal was described as writing our own bible or sacred story. The diary or daily journal was described in chapter 4 as a place in which many writers have kept steady records of their experiences with God. Other writers have discovered that writing the story of their past spiritual journey or relationship with the Holy One has been useful in tracing their own religious development.

Many journal writers have used the journal or diary for other ways of encountering the divine. Some simply pray their experiences in writing. Writing about these encounters provided the main motivation for Nancy Mairs' memoir, *Ordinary Time*:

God is here. And here, and here, and here. Not an immutable entity detached from time but a continual calling and coming into being. Not transcendence, . . . but immanence: God working out Godself in every thing. Process, yes, that's what I want to explore and celebrate, the holy as verb, Godding, not Godness or Godhood. . . . I'm certain that God slips and surprises more gloriously than Gerard Manley Hopkin's stippled trout.

Others actually write prayers each day. Some write dialogues with the Creator, while others use the journal as a place to record their reflections on biblical passages or other readings that have proven helpful for their journey. Whichever form the writing takes, the journal can be a place of prayer and meditation because in it the diarist responds to an awareness of the sacred Presence.

"Moments in which we **drink deeply** from the source of meaning are **moments of prayer**, whether we call them so or not."

David Steindl-Rast

Write!

Elizabeth Roberts and Elias Amidon offer this advice about sacred writing: "You find a moment. . . . You open the journal, pausing to recollect where you have been and who you are becoming. It is as if between the covers of your journal you enter place of spiritual retreat and contemplation, much as a nun or monk enters her or his simple cell. Here the rapid flow of daily business is left outside. In the private world of your journal a sense of spaciousness unfolds, held in focus by the thoughtful movements of your pen on the page." This kind of sacred flow-writing simply records awareness of the Spirit's pervasive presence in nature, people, and other experiences. If you only wrote this kind of reflection, this praying of experiences, you would have a profound experience of the Divine. Try praying your experiences in flow-writing.

Journal Prayers

The move from praying our experiences to writing prayers is only a short step. In all religious traditions, four kinds of prayer emerge, and they arise from the very human need to say thanks, give praise, beg forgiveness, and ask for help. Writing such prayers gives concrete form and substance to interaction with the Holy One. Writing the prayer also leaves a record of our story with the Creator, those important moments of interaction. All sacred literature preserves ancestral prayers. Generations of Jews and Christians continue to offer the psalms. Monks and the devout recite verses from the Hindu sacred books. When a diarist writes her or his prayers, she or he is simply doing what those unknown spiritual ancestors did, recording these responses to God's presence as a testament of faith, hope, and love.

> "The presence of God is like the atmosphere we breathe."
>
> *Thomas Keating*

Gratitude. All of life, each moment, is a gift from the Creator of life. Gratitude is the most natural response to the daily gifts. As with any prayer, prayers of gratitude begin in awareness of the gifts. In his famous journal written in the mid-1700s, Quaker abolitionist John Woolman opened with these lines: "I have often felt a motion of love to leave some hints in writing of my experience of the goodness of God, and now, in the thirty-sixth year of my age, I begin this work." Woolman conceived of his entire journal as thanksgiving for the Creator's gifts that Woolman pondered with eyes of wonder. The journal invites writers to do the same today.

One way of beginning the prayer of gratitude is by listing the blessings of the day. After reading *Simple Abundance*, Oprah Winfrey helped popularize Sarah Ban Breathnach's practice of keeping a daily gratitude journal in which we thoughtfully bring all the blessings of the day into our awareness and write each one down on the page. In itself, recording the lists of blessings expands our awareness both of the world of giftedness and of the Spirit's presence. The lists are often filled with wonderful surprises. In his book *Gratefulness*, Benedictine monk, David Steindl-Rast advises: "What counts on your path to fulfillment is that we remember the great truth that moments of surprise want to teach us: everything is gratuitous, everything is gift. The degree to which we are awake to this truth is the measure of our gratefulness. And gratefulness is the measure of our aliveness." The lists alone become an ancient form of prayer, a litany, declaring our surprise and joy at the gifts and a sign of our aliveness. When we simply add a phrase like "Thank you, Holy Friend," the list becomes more explicitly a psalm of gratitude.

Another form that gratitude can take are personal songs or psalms of gratitude. The biblical psalms are filled with songs of thanksgiving. For example, Psalm 136 provides a pattern for prayers of gratitude:

I give thanks to you, Creator, for you are good!
Your love will last forever.
You alone do wondrous deeds!
Your love will last forever.
You created the great lights in the heavens!
Your love will last forever. . . .

The composer of the psalm does what poets and hymn writers have done since, describe a miracle of the Creator's art and then repeat words of thanks and praise.

Expressing gratitude doesn't add anything to the glory of the Holy One. People offer thanksgiving to recognize their right place in the scheme of things; that is, human beings are the beneficiaries of abundant giftedness. People also give thanks for the good of their own souls. In putting words to thanksgiving, they remind themselves that there are reasons for hope and joy. Even hiding from the Nazis, Anne Frank could write in her diary:

> When I lie in bed and end my prayers with the words, 'I thank you, God, for all that is good and dear and beautiful,' I am filled with joy. Then I think about 'the good' of going into hiding, of my health. . . and of 'the beauty' which exists in the world. . . . Look at these things, then you find yourself again, and God, and then you regain your balance.

Writing our thanks does help us regain our perspective and opens up an avenue to joy.

Confession. Acknowledging failures, confessing our shortcomings, seeking forgiveness are all part of any relationship and a life of prayer. We move out of harmony with our desire to love. We cease living from the core of our beliefs. We need to start over and put life back in right relation. As twelve-step programs of all kinds understand, this move back to balance often starts with us acknowledging or confessing when we have missed the mark, that we need help in directing our life in new ways.

In her diary, Catherine de Hueck Doherty, who became known for her great charity, wrote this prayer of confession:

> Beloved, I try so hard, but somehow I never seem to succeed. I work so hard at Your works of mercy, but I seem to have no charity. Efficiency, kindness, goodness of heart—yes. But I have nothing like real charity—that elusive tenderness and sensitivity to the feelings of others that mark true charity.
>
> . . . For the sake of Your poor and unfortunate children, give it to me, Beloved. Light my soul with the gift of prayer. Give me an understanding and practice of humility. Have mercy on me, Master!

Catherine de Hueck Doherty's prayer confesses her regret and pleads for help, the pattern of the prayer of confession. She confronts the truth: We are not whole, and only the aid of our Higher Power can make us so.

Petition. Asking God for help may be the most frequent prayer offered by human beings. Children ask God to "keep" their souls as they sleep. As they bite their nails, anxious fans at a state high school championship game storm the heavens, begging that their team pulls off a stunning upset. Parents pray for the safety of their children. Elders ask for healing. Indeed, few humans are unfamiliar with petitionary prayer.

Most petitionary prayer springs from a human need, but also from an image of a Higher Power as provider, caregiver, and friend or parent. By asking for what they need, people are expressing trust in the relationship. Seeking help is in effect like saying: "I trust you and need you." Petitioners acknowledge their dependence on God and remember that every gift, even life, comes from the Creator. Even popes ask God for help. In *Journal of a Soul,* beloved Pope John XXIII wrote the following prayer on August 14, 1961:

> O Jesus, here I am before you. You are suffering and dying for me, old as I am now and drawing near to the end of my service and my life. Hold me closely, and near to your heart, letting mine beat with yours. I love to feel myself bound for ever to you with a gold chain, woven of lovely, delicate links.

> The first link: the justice which obliges me to find my God wherever I turn.

> The second link: the providence and goodness which will guide my feet.

The third link: love for my neighbor, unwearying and most patient.

Like all truly humble people, Pope John knew that he too relied on the help of his God. His journal is filled with these poignant expressions of his need.

John and members of the Christian community believe that God invites their cries for help. In the gospel of Matthew, Jesus says: "Ask, and it will be given to you; search, and you will find; knock, and the door will be opened for you. For everyone who asks receives, and everyone who searches finds, and for everyone who knocks, the door will be opened." Muslims, Jews, and followers of other religious traditions likewise ask for divine help. They likewise believe in God's providence and love of humanity.

People not only write prayers for themselves, but often intercede for other people. One of the most common prayers is for healing. People do not pray that God has a change of mind and decides to cure someone out of a sudden love of the person. Healing prayer begins with faith that God already loves all of humanity. Healing prayer can change our own relationship with God and with the person we are praying for. Prayer creates a bond with that person that may not have been there before. We allow ourselves, indeed commit ourselves, to be a channel of God's love for the other person. The healing that occurs may not be exactly according to our agenda, but healing happens.

After conducting research about the power of prayer to heal, physician Larry Dossey concluded, "The power of love to change bodies is legendary, built into folklore, common sense, and everyday experience." Now that power is being documented in scientific studies. Books by medical doctors and researchers supporting the curative power of intercessory prayer include: *Healing Words: The Power of Prayer and the Practice of Medicine*; *Prayer Is Good Medicine: How to Reap the Healing Benefits of Prayer*; *Timeless Healing: The Power and Biology of Belief*; and *Love and Survival*. Science is catching up with belief. Writing prayers for healing makes tangible and vivid our cares and hopes for the good of those in need.

Praise. In her book about prayer, *When in Doubt, Sing*, Jane Redmont remarks, "Experiences of peace, ecstasy, satisfaction, or creativity can in themselves be a prayer . . . or can lead to prayer: witnessing a child's first steps, making love, putting in the garden for the season." These moments of joy cause words of praise to bubble up. Writing them down testifies to, tells the story of, these times of wonder and happiness. When darkness seems to pervade our life, reading these stories of joy can provide solace and hope.

Writing prayers of praise takes discipline for many people. So much of what passes as news is strictly bad news: murders and wrecks, epidemics and scandals, tornadoes and lawsuits. We're fed a steady diet of bad news. The joyful stories are ones we must tell ourselves, hold onto, and remember in order to maintain our balance. A spiritual practice of recording and exulting in these moments of joy takes conscious commitment.

Writing praise need not be complicated, though. Dan Wakefield, author of books on memoir writing, tells of an early experience learning praise when he was just starting to journal:

> I meditated while looking at a blade of grass for twenty minutes every day for two weeks and was amazed that I kept seeing something new all the time . . . the *aliveness* of it. I wrote in my notebook . . . the words that seemed to describe th qualities of God as He manifested Himself in the grass He created: "tenacious," "resilient," "alive," "communicating," "dancing," "dependent," "surprising," "reaching," "responding."

Each of these words is a prayer of praise because each one recognizes and honors an aspect of the Creator. The words depend on being aware of the grass as manifesting God and then each one is a response to that awareness.

Prayers of praise correspond well with Wordsworth's definition of poetry as "the spontaneous overflow of powerful emotion." This overflow is evident in this prayer from Teresa of Avila's *Autobiography*:

May everything created, O Lord of all the world, praise You and bless You! If only I could tramp the whole world over, proclaiming everywhere with all the strength that is in me what a faithful friend You are to those who will be friends with You! . . . O my Lord, how kindly, how nobly, how tenderly, how sweetly You succeed in handling and making sure of Your own!

Teresa wrote this prayer during a time of great suffering. It was a way of pushing back despair and holding fast to joy. Writing the prayer worked for her and has for others for generations.

"Let nothing disturb you, Let nothing frighten you, Though all things pass **God does not change.** Patience wins all things. But they lack nothing Who possess God; **For God alone suffices.**"

Teresa of Avila

Write!

Writing prayers of gratitude, confession, petition, and praise is best done spontaneously after a period of sitting in awareness.

- So, breathe deeply. Open your senses to awareness of what is around you. Listen to the stirrings of your own heart.

- If you find it helpful, write lists of things for which you are be grateful, failures for which you have regrets, your needs and those of others, and moments of joy. Just writing the lists can be a prayer of awareness.

- If you feel moved, pour out your thanks, confessions, petitions, and praise freely and with complete honesty.

- End with an Amen or maybe Alleluia.

Dialogues and Letters

J ust as dialogues play an essential role in relationships with other people, they play the same role in relationship with the Spirit. We converse with the sacred Spirit who lives inside everything, including the human heart. We listen and respond, carrying on the sort of conversation that we have with a beloved. Such conversations have been recorded from ancient days until the present.

Abraham, Moses, all the prophets talked with God. Moses even debated with God about his choice to lead the people out of slavery, raising objection after objection:

> Moses: Who am I that I should go to Pharaoh, and bring the Israelites out of Egypt?
>
> God: I will be with you.
>
> Moses: If I come to the Israelites and say to them, "The God of your ancestors has sent me to you," and they ask me, "What is God's name?" what shall I say to them?
>
> God: I AM WHO I AM.

And so on. Granted, Moses believed that God spoke to him because the voice came from the burning bush. He also knew it was God because God's words would only lead to good for the people. And, indeed, knowing what is from God and what is not is important.

The true test of words from the Holy is this: Will the consequences of these words lead me to love more fully and inclusively? If the listener-writer believes that the Spirit of God dwells inside him or her and the message from the Spirit challenges him or her to love and do good, then those words can be taken into the heart and flow into action. The mystic Catherine of Siena carried on long dialogues with God, which were recorded by a friar and confidant and collected in a volume called *The Dialogue* that is read even today, centuries later. In this dialogue, God makes clear that love and how we are to love are at the core of all divine communication:

> I [God] ask you to love me with the same love with which I love you. . . . I love you not out of duty but gratuitously. So you cannot give me the kind of love I ask of you. This is why I have put you among your neighbors: so that you can do for them what you cannot do for me—that is, love them without any concern for thanks. . . . And whatever you do for them I will consider done for me.

The same kind of invitation to dialogue is always given to us.

Etty Hillesum, a young Dutch woman who died in a Nazi concentration camp, kept a diary of her last years. With

the threat of annihilation hanging over her, she kept her
Spirit alive by her journal. Dialogues with God were a key
part. On August 18, 1943, she wrote:

> You have made me so rich, oh God, please let me
> share out Your beauty with open hands. My life
> has become an uninterrupted dialogue with You,
> oh God, one great dialogue. Sometimes when I
> stand in some corner of the camp, my feet
> planted on Your earth, my eyes raised towards
> Your Heaven, tears sometimes run down my face,
> tears of deep emotion and gratitude. . . . All my
> creative powers are translated into inner
> dialogues with You; the beat of my heart has
> grown deeper, more active and yet more
> peaceful.

Until her death in the gas chambers, these dialogues
sustained and nourished Hillesum.

Such dialogues have done the same for the countless
diarists that have entered into them with faith and an open
heart. Writing a dialogue with the Holy One is easy. One
can begin with a question like Moses did, listen, and then
write the response. The dialogue can continue from there.

Writing dialogues with God may feel uncomfortable, but
the same sort of listening and responding may be
accomplished by writing letters to the Creator. Honest and
open letters to God help writers listen to their own heart's

> **"In the center** and the middle [of the soul] is the main dwelling place where the **very secret exchanges** between God and the soul take place."

Teresa of Avila

deepest longings and inner wisdom. In Alice Walker's novel, *The Color Purple*, Celie has no human being with whom she can pour out her grief, her passions, her fears, and so she—like so many writers before her—writes letters to God. Her first letter begins this way:

Dear God,

I am fourteen years old. . . . I have always been a good girl. Maybe you can give me a sign letting me know what is happening to me.

Celie has to talk to someone, and God is her only option. As with many conversations, hers begins with a question. In writing to God, she will come to find the answers as her own Spirit speaks. God knows what is in each human heart. The letters tell the writer what is there and what is of the Spirit.

Write!

- Begin your dialogue by simply addressing God in whatever manner is comfortable for you, perhaps starting with a question. Then take a breath, pause, listen, and let God speak back to you through your pen. Write down what comes and let the dialogue flow where it will.

- Letters to God can open like Celie's: "Dear God." Then pour out whatever needs to be said at the time. Remember that these letters to God are not communiqués in which you need to take God's feelings into account. God knows your feelings and thoughts anyway. Letting the letter ramble and move freely proves most helpful.

"Some **keep the Sabbath** going to Church–I keep it, staying at Home–**With a Bobolink** for a Chorister–And an Orchard, for a Dome. . . . God preaches, a noted Clergyman–And the sermon is never long, So instead of getting to **Heaven,** at last–I'm going, all along."

Emily Dickinson

Reflections on Sacred Reading

Many diarists include writing their reflections about reading that they are doing. Priest, sociologist, and novelist Andrew Greeley kept prayer journals for several years. Many of these entries, all addressed to God, were composed of his response to passages from biblical texts or other readings, like this one:

February 13, 1993 – Tucson

My Love,

Qohelet tells us this morning how hard it is to find a good woman, but he adds that it is also hard to find a good man. Then characteristically he says that it is all absurdity anyway. In effect he's saying that. Your ways are mysterious, especially in the man/woman relationship. . . . You have made the genders sufficiently different as to be attractive to one another and at the same time so different as to drive each other up the wall. . . .

Yet love is stronger than death and even more so is Love.

For Greeley and all who read sacred texts for instruction and inspiration, writing reflections on what the Spirit speaks to them is a natural response.

The practice of reading and responding has traditionally been called *lectio divina* or holy study. Writing reflections on sacred texts, dialogues, letters, prayers, or spontaneous praying of experiences are all ways of visiting with God. This written record honors the communication and, over time, provides a vivid story of our relationship with the Ground of All Being.

"What I want to achieve, what I have been striving and pining to achieve these thirty years, is self-realization, to see God face to face. . . . All that I do by way of speaking and writing, and all my ventures in the political field, are directed to this same end."

Mohandas Gandhi

"**This Spirit** of **truth** abides with you and will be in you. The Advocate, the **Holy Spirit,** will teach you everything. **Do not** let **your hearts** be **troubled."**

Gospel of John

The process of *lectio divina* may be done with any brief text. Following its steps allows deeper insight and a more profound experience of a passage we may have read many times. This type of journal writing has sustained many people on their spiritual journeys and certainly recommends itself for those who find sacred reading an important component of their relationship with the Holy.

Write!

Take some time to practice sacred reading: Spiritual teachers have offered a variety of ways to do **lectio divina,** but most include the following steps:

1. **Lectio** usually begins with a time to center and relax in silence, recalling the Spirit within.

2. Slowly, read a short passage from a sacred text, a poem, or book of meditations. Let your heart taste the words and allow your consciousness to focus on certain words or a phrase that invites special attention.

3. Next, interiorly repeat over and over again the one line that seems to be especially important until its import becomes clear. Some diarists even write the phrase in their journal at this point.

4. Read the passage a second time, slowly and attentively.

5. Let your mind and heart formulate a one word or short phrase response to the reading. This word or phrase may be written down and then silently recited in harmony with your breathing.

6. Slowly, read the passage one last time.

7. After a time of quiet pondering, write your reflections with this question in mind: How does this reading touch my life at this particular time?

   Lectio divina usually ends with a quiet period, a prayer, or just thoughts of thankfulness.

chapternine

Looking**Forward**

"Allow yourself a space of quiet. . . . Nowhere can a man find a quieter or more untroubled **retreat than in his own soul. . . .** Avail yourself often, then, of this retirement, and so continually **renew yourself."**

Marcus Aurelius

Eyes on the Prize

One of the central points of this book is this: Spiritual maturation, the movement toward wholeness, begins with self-appropriation (understanding and acceptance) and leads to self-transcendence. Most of the journal writing described to this point has been directed towards self-appropriation and that is at it should be. It's next to impossible to know where we are going without knowing, understanding, and owning where we are and where we have been. However, most journal writers come to a place at which they want to look outward and forward.

One practice that many journal writers use to look outward and forward is writing their own mission statement: a brief, focused expression of the central goal of their life. Viktor Frankl, concentration camp survivor and author of *Man's Search for Meaning*, commented: "Everyone has his own specific vocation or mission in life: everyone must carry out a concrete assignment that demands fulfillment. Therein he cannot be replaced, nor his life repeated. Thus, everyone's task is as unique as his special opportunity to implement it." Composing this mission helps us tap into our unique dignity, responsibility, and calling: our vocation. This guiding sense of vocation can draw us forward.

Meditation teacher Jon Kabat-Zinn suggests posing this question to ourselves in order to arrive at some sense of our mission: "What is my job on the planet?" There are really two elements to explore in the question. First, what is *my job?* Not anyone else's, but the job that is given only to me. Like writers before him, Kabat-Zinn understands that many people waste much of their lives doing someone else's job, trying to meet other people's expectations, listening to a cacophony of voices all telling them who they should be and what they should do. A person's job is the JOB, all capital, the JOB that only she or he can do.

Buckminster Fuller asked himself this question to uncover his JOB: "What is it on this planet that needs doing that I know something about, that probably won't happen unless I take responsibility for it?" The JOB each person has is more than the paid employment that he or she does; that may be part of the JOB, but probably only a part. Parenting their particular children is part of any parents' JOB. An aspect of a waiter's JOB might be to bring his unique brand of politeness to his diners. A heart surgeon's JOB might include her special way of careful listening that she offers each patient. By uncovering their particular talents, gifts, skills, and stories in writing, diarists begin to understand and appropriate many of the qualities that are part of their JOB.

The second part of Kabat-Zinn's question is equally important and suggests the dignity that comes from embracing our JOB: "What is my job *on the planet?*" One awareness that the ecological movement has brought to us is a sharper realization that all elements—everything—on the planet and in the universe are connected. Planting trees in Alabama makes the planet greener—not just the plot of earth near Tuscaloosa. An oil spill off Spain has consequences that reach farther away than one stretch of coastline. A friendly, helpful clerk at a hardware store—someone doing her JOB well—makes the day brighter not only for her customer but probably for the customer's family. A nursing home resident who sees his JOB as smiling at others because a stroke has slurred his speech makes life easier for the nurses aide who bathes him, making her day better.

Our JOB is on and for the planet. "Working for humanity as an employee of the universe at large," Kabat-Zinn remarks, "you get to modify and contribute to your locale by who you are, how you are, and what you do. But it's no longer personal. It's just part of the totality of the universe expressing itself." How a person uniquely contributes to the planet is his or her mission, his or her JOB.

Writing mission statements has become ubiquitous in businesses, schools, and organizations of all kinds. Too often mission statements are grab bags of high sounding verbiage meant to put a good face on business-as-usual. When organizations do use them to direct and motivate their members, mission statements can keep everyone's eyes on the prize. Henry Ford's mission statement, "to democratize the automobile," certainly revolutionized the auto industry by giving the world the Model T, an affordable, dependable car for the masses.

But mission statements have inspired and focused individuals as well. Consider these:

1. Jesus offered his mission statement this way: "The Spirit is upon me . . . to bring the good news to the poor . . . to proclaim release to the captives and recovery of sight to the blind, to let the oppressed go free" (Luke 4:18).

2. Having been a mercenary soldier, Ignatius of Loyola underwent a conversion while recuperating from horrible wounds received in battle. One fruit of his time of convalescence was this mission statement that he wrote later: "God's purpose in creating us is to draw forth from us a response of love and service here on earth."

> "I know of no more encouraging fact than the unquestionable ability of man to elevate his life by conscious endeavor."
>
> *Henry David Thoreau*

3. In 1961, Pope John XXIII wrote his mission statement in his journal: "Considering the purpose of my own life I must:

    1. Desire only to be virtuous and holy, and so be pleasing to God.

    2. Direct all things, thoughts as well as actions, to the increase, the service and the glory of the Holy Church.

    3. Recognize that I have been set here by God, and therefore remain perfectly serene about all that happens, not only as regards myself but also with regard to the Church, continuing to work and suffer with Christ, for her good.

    4. Entrust myself at all times to Divine Providence."

4. Thea Bowman, an African-American sister, human rights activist, and teacher, gave inspirational speeches all over the world even while slowly dying of cancer. She once described what kept her going this way: "My prayer has become, 'Lord, let me live until I die.' By that I mean I want to live, love, and serve fully until death comes."

The journal is a perfect place to look forward and outward. To do this, journal keepers have written mission statements—even though they may never have named them that. Nevertheless, somewhere in each journal or memoir the writer seeks to answer the question: "What is my job on the planet?"

Write!

To write a personal mission statement, you would do well to review your entries, trying to renew your sense of your giftedness, skills, desires, hopes, experiences—what truly gives you joy and nurtures love. You might also challenge yourself with this advice from Annie Dillard: "There is always an enormous temptation in all of life to diddle around making itsy-bitsy friends and meals and journeys for itsy-bitsy years on end. . . . And then sulk along the rest of your days on the edge of rage. I won't have it. The world is wilder than that in all directions, more dangerous and bitter, more extravagant and bright. We are making hay when we should be making whoopee; we are raising tomatoes when we should be raising Cain, or Lazarus."

With these things in mind, free-write in answer to the question "What is my job on the planet?" This can lead to many insights.

Take a few days away from the exercise and then review all your ideas, usually one or two key points will stand out. These core values or goals can form a personal mission statement. Try to write your mission statement in one or two sentences at most.

Note well: Like corporate mission statements, personal mission statements wither from lack of use. They also need periodic tending, pruning, and renewing.

Discerning Ways

Journals have always been places in which thoughtful people have discerned what to do, which way to go, and what decision will be in closest alignment with their beliefs. In his biography of Roman Emperor Marcus Aurelius, Brand Blanshard says, "When the camp had gone to sleep, the emperor . . . sat at his table and took stock, not of battles, sieges, and fortunes, of which there is little mention, but of himself, his state of mind, his lapses from justice or from speaking the truth or from command of his temper. He used these night hours to conjure up the ideals he had set before himself as a man and as a ruler of men, to see them more clearly." The Emperor's discernment led him to more thoughtful and wise choices, especially when compared to his predecessors and successors on the throne. Marcus Aurelius recorded his discernment in his *Meditations* (see chapter 2).

> ## "Nothing unless first a dream."
>
> *Carl Sandburg*

Modern leaders likewise discern important matters in their journals. Trappist monk Thomas Merton, perhaps the most influential spiritual writer of the twentieth century, wrote this entry in his journal of September 13, 1952:

I have been making decisions.

The chief of these is that I must really lead a solitary life. It is not enough to try to be a solitary in community. Too much ambivalence. Wednesday—a conference with Fr. Bellarmine. He is the first person who has ever told me point blank that I belonged in a Charterhouse and *not* at Gethsemani [his monastery].

As soon as he said it, I saw that he was completely right and everything inside me affirmed it by peace and happiness. . . .

Wrote to Dom Humphrey at Sky Farm . . . everything sure and serene. Praying a lot. I feel that my desire for solitude is now the one thing that most unites me to God. Prayer in hope— swimming in the Holy Ghost and at the same time utterly pure. The hope alone is wonderful.

Even though Merton seemed sure here, his discernment took many years, and it is all reflected in later journal entries. In fact, Merton stayed at his monastery but lived in a hermitage. What the writing did for Merton—as it does for all diarists—was help him understand the elements of his decision, reflect on his feelings of inner rightness or discomfort in the decision, and explore alternatives.

Having a written record allowed Merton and Marcus Aurelius to go back, review what they had said, and revise and expand on their thoughts and feelings.

Discernment, the process Merton and Marcus Aurelius used, is different than using a good decision-making process that involves gathering all the facts, considering and ordering the pros and cons, looking at consequences and cost-benefit analysis, and then making a decision. Discernment invites people to consider the full range of their experiences, thoughts, and feelings around an issue. Matters of the heart play a much greater role in the process of discernment than in traditional decision-making procedures.

An essential element in discernment is to pay attention to how we feel. Jane Redmont quotes a Jesuit priest's understanding of how Ignatius of Loyola discerned: "He was noticing and paying attention to what he was feeling inside. If we notice each day where we feel consolation, we *become discerning people* rather than *going through a process of discernment.* If we are noticing where and how God is acting in our lives each day, we will become more aware of the choices we need to keep making that fit with God's activity." Using a discernment process to journal about a decision can lead to better understanding, but a regular practice of listening to our heart in the pages of our journal helps us grow into discerning people.

In her book, *Women at the Well*, Kathleen Fischer suggests eight guides to discerning. These are adapted here in the form of questions that can be used for discernment in journal writing:

1. *What does your deepest self seem to be telling you?* Often we fail to listen to the voices of our heart. So many outside voices tell us to do this or that, so we may not be listening carefully enough to the "still, small voice" of our own heart.

2. *What are my needs in this situation, as well as the needs of other people?* Certainly the legitimate needs of the "planet" should be part of any discernment, but so should our own legitimate needs. Merton was not insensitive to his brother monks at Gethsemani, but he had to listen to his need for more solitude too.

3. *Am I just being passive or is this the will of the Holy One?* Fischer wisely points out that people can "mistakenly think they are living out God's will when they are merely living out of a cultural pattern of conformity or helplessness." She also advises that people should be cautious in thinking that God has an exact blueprint of how they should act. Beyond loving the Creator and loving others as we love ourselves, God's plan is seldom exact.

4. *What insights are coming from my body, intuition, and feelings?* Reason is not all it's cracked up to be. It can help us in discernment, but ignoring the messages from our body, our intuition, and feelings places us at

risk for making decisions out of harmony with what is most true to our JOB on the planet.

5. *What are the social and cultural forces at work in this situation?* We are interconnected to all people and all elements of creation. They must be taken into account. In addition, Fischer says, "Approaches to discernment need to be based on the realization that healing society's inequities is the only lasting way to bring about spiritual wholeness for all persons."

6. *How has my social conditioning influenced my feelings about this situation?* When we discern, we are concerned primarily about what our Spirit calls us to do and *be*. Our social conditioning may be at war with the Spirit. If we have been tracking our experiences in the journal, we will likely be more aware of these social influences.

7. *What are all the alternatives that could lead to fuller life?* Brainstorming as many possibilities for action always broadens our perspective.

8. *What will be the consequences, gains, and losses of the changes I want to make?* Any choice means letting some things go. Decisions also have an array of consequences, gains, and losses. These all need to be clearly scrutinized in the journal.

When all these questions have been examined with head, heart, and body, then we might be ready to make a decision. Having discerned meditatively and fully, we are more likely to make a decision that will be life giving and aligned with our deepest values and our JOB on the planet.

"Go to your bosom: Knock there, and **ask your heart** what it doth know."

William Shakespeare

Write.

Any diarist trying to discern an issue would be well served by Fischer's eight questions. Try to describe and explore each issue. Some clarity will emerge in the process, but some issues defy blueprint answers.

Nurturing Wisdom

One aid in keeping focused on our mission and broadening our perspective during discernment is to keep an ongoing store of wisdom drawn from other sources: favorite quotes, sayings, and articles. Many diarists record these wise sayings in their journals for soul-nourishment at some point in the future.

Collections of a person's important wisdom literature are called "commonplace books." In the Bible, the Book of Proverbs is a collection of adages and maxims, a commonplace book. Such collections were quite popular in the 1700s and 1800s. While the collectors of these sayings used them as inspiration while they were alive, these collections offered a lot of insight into the person later on.

> **"Freedom** is what you do with what's been **done to you."**
>
> *Jean-Paul Sartre*

In his 1992 memoir *PrairyErth*, William Least Heat-Moon included a section called "From the Commonplace Book" in each chapter. About these storehouses of quotes, he remarked: "If you gather them over a lifetime, you can look back and say, 'This is what I thought was important when I was twenty. . . .' It really reveals ourselves to

> "**Learning** is not attained by chance; it must be sought for with ardor and attended to **with diligence.**"

Abigail Adams

ourselves." Doris Grumbach's book *The Presence of Absence* is both memoir and a commonplace book in which she records sayings that were important to her during the period in which the book was written. Here are few of the entries:

Add to thoughts on pain: Somewhere, Theophan, the Russian bishop and recluse, said, "The awareness of God shall be with you as clearly as a toothache."

Shortest instruction ever given on prayer: St. Paul advised the Thessalonians to "pray without ceasing" (I.12:17).

Thomas Kelly, adding to my catalogue of using the senses to approach God: "Lead a *listening* life. Order your outward life so that nothing drowns out the listening."

Simone Weil: "Religion is nothing more than a looking."

For Least Heat-Moon and Grumbach, these commonplace book sections of the journal look forward, but they also helped them look back.

Write.

Consider creating a special section in your journal exclusively for your own "commonplace book." While it is not necessary to include the full source citation for quotes, people who speak in public, teach, or write find including the book title and page number of the quote handy for later reference. Mostly though, the commonplace book is meant for inspiration as life's journey unfolds.

> "When you come to the **edge of all the light** you have, and must take a step into the darkness of the unknown, believe that one of two things will happen. Either there will be something solid for you to stand on—or you will be taught **how to fly.**"
>
> *Patrick Overton*

Generating Possibilities

Finally, many diarists use their journals as workbooks to generate new ideas and plan. While much of the work of the journal might seem serious, and often is, the journal can also be a place of dreams, visions, and play. The great baseball player Satchel Paige, who lived to a great old age quipped, "We don't stop playing because we grow old, we grow old because we stop playing." Many new ideas may come out in the daily journal as we flow write. Other notions that we want to explore can come from looking at the past. Journal writers are always generating new avenues of adventure. As J. Robert Oppenheimer remarked, "Discovery follows discovery; each both raising and answering questions; each ending a long search, and each providing the new instruments for a new search."

Keep in mind these three ways of generating possibilities.

Lists. Making lists is a helpful practice for looking at the past or the future. Here are some lists that can generate energy for the future:

- Ten small changes in my life
- Several changes I want to make in my work
- Ten things I want to do before I die
- Twenty wishes: Start each sentence with "I wish . . ."
- People with whom I want to spend more time
- People with whom I want to spend less time
- Complete this sentence as many times as you can: "In the future I want God to . . ."
- Complete this sentence as many times as you can: "In the future, I think God wants me to . . ."
- Hobbies that sound interesting
- Courses or continuing education classes that attract me
- Five skills that would be great to have
- Some things that I used to enjoy doing, stopped, but could start again

Mind-Map. Mind-mapping or clustering is another technique for generating ideas. See the Write! exercise in chapter 4, on page 82, for an illustrated explanation of this process.

Tree of Possibilities. This is a technique that some fiction writers use to generate plot ideas, but it also works for other purposes. The process goes like this:

- At the top of a page, the diarist writes a sentence for which she or he wants to generate possibilities: for example, "I want to learn to play the recorder."

- Below this, she or he writes three possible alternatives: for example,

Talk to Mary Ellen, Check out WWTC, See if the U. has lessons

Then she or he generates three possible actions for each of these three alternatives. For example, for Check out WWTC:

Call for class schedule, Call music department, Call Terri

And so on. In other words, a tree forms from the top. Each idea creates three more ideas. Eventually, we select a course of action based on this tree of possibilities.

Write!

Try listing, mind-mapping or clustering, and using the tree of possibilities to start creative juices flowing, rev up your optimism, and help you launch into new adventures. Satchel Paige's advice about staying young by playing can urge us on to creativity in looking outward and forward.

> **"The spiritual life** is not a quick sprint to a well-marked finish line, but a marathon, an arduous **lifelong journey** into an ever-widening horizon."

Ronald Rolheiser

Final Words

This book opened by describing the phenomenon of journal and memoir writing. Millions of people find that writing their personal story is therapeutic, freeing, and balancing. While many ways of journal writing have been described, journal writers find their own way of keeping the diary or constructing their memoir. Knowing all the ways of writing offers a writer a helpful choice of tools. Anyone trying to build anything—even a richer spiritual life—needs just the right tools for certain tasks.

While the main purpose of the book was to supply information about writing for the soul, actually keeping a journal is the only way of really understanding and profiting from writing. So, please, write. Exploring our life, accepting our story, discovering our gifts, discerning life's persistent questions, and looking forward are wonderful for the writer, but also the planet.

"A journal is always a self-portrait, it's narrative still evolving. The story of any living diarist's life is in flux, its ending yet to be written."

Alexandra Johnson

RecommendedReading:
10FavoriteGuidesto
Journaland
MemoirWriting

1. Christina Baldwin. *Life's Companion: Journal Writing as a Spiritual Quest.* Bantam, 1990.

2. Annie Dillard. *The Writing Life.* Harper & Row, 1989.

3. Peter Gilmour. *The Wisdom of Memoir: Reading and Writing Life's Sacred Texts.* Saint Mary's Press, 1997.

4. Alexandra Johnson. *Leaving a Trace: On Keeping a Journal.* Back Bay, 2002.

5. John Kotre. *White Gloves: How We Create Ourselves Through Memory.* Free Press, 1995.

6. Denis Ledoux. *Turning Memories into Memoirs: A Handbook for Writing Lifestories.* Soleil Press, 1993.

7. Ira Progoff. *At a Journal Workshop.* Dialogue House, 1975.

8. Marlene A. Schiwy. *A Voice of Her Own: Women and the Journal Writing Journey.* Simon & Schuster, 1996.

9. Ilene Segalove & Paul Bob Velick. *List Your Self: Listmaking as the Way to Self Discovery.* Andrews McMeel, 1996.

10. Dan Wakefield. *The Story of Your Life: Writing a Spiritual Autobiography.* Beacon Press, 1990.

10 Favorite Diaries or Journals

1. Anne Frank. *The Diary of a Young Girl.* Doubleday, 1952.

2. Jon Hassler. *My Staggerford Journal.* Ballantine, 1999.

3. Etty Hillesum. *An Interrupted Life: The Diaries of Etty Hillesum, 1941–1943.* trans. by Arno Pomerans. Pantheon, 1983.

4. Pope John XXIII. *Journal of a Soul.* McGraw-Hill, 1965.

5. Madeleine L'Engle. *A Circle of Quiet.* HarperSanFrancisco, 1972.

6. Audre Lorde. *The Cancer Journals.* Spinsters/Aunt Lute Books, 1980.

7. Thomas Merton. *The Intimate Merton: His Life from His Journals.* Ed. by Patrick Hart & Jonathan Montaldo. HarperSanFrancisco, 1995.

8. Henri J.M. Nouwen. *The Genesee Diary.* Doubleday, 1976.

9. May Sarton. *Journal of a Solitude.* Norton, 1992.

10. Virginia Woolf. *A Writer's Diary.* Harcourt, 1953.

10 Favorite Memoirs

1. Russell Baker. *Growing Up.* New American Library, 1983.

2. Frederick Buechner. *The Sacred Journey.* Harper & Row, 1982.

3. Susan Cahill, ed. *Writing Women's Lives.* HarperPerennial, 1994.

4. Nien Cheng. *Life and Death in Shanghai.* Penguin, 1988.

5. Jill Ker Conway, ed. *Written by Herself.* Vols. 1 & 2. Vintage Books.

6. Doris Grumbach. *The Presence of Absence.* Beacon Press, 1998.

7. Margaret E. Murie. *Two in the Far North.* Alaska Northwest Books, 1957, 1997.

8. Kathleen Norris. *Dakota: A Spiritual Geography.* Houghton-Mifflin, 1993.

9. Dan Wakefield. *Returning: A Spiritual Journey.* Doubleday, 1988.

10. Elie Wiesel. *Night.* Avon, 1960.

CARL KOCH currently serves as an adjunct professor at the Graduate School of Saint Mary's University in Minnesota, teaching in the Master of Arts Human Development program and the Doctor of Education Leadership program. He has authored and edited many books on prayer and spirituality, including high school textbooks. He and his wife, Joyce Heil, live in Onalaska, Wisconsin.

Exploring A Great Spiritual Practice

Meditation:
Exploring A Great Spiritual Practice
Richard Chilson, author
John Kirvan, Series Editor

Explore meditation as a spiritual practice. Packed with information drawn from a wide variety of religious traditions, this reader-friendly guide features "how-tos," images, inspirational quotes, and an extensive glossary.

ISBN:1-893732-73-8
256 pages / $13.95

ISBN:1-893732-67-3
224 pages / $12.95

NEW SERIES!
Exploring a Great Spiritual Practice—
reader friendly books with a world vision, credible information, practical advice, and easy to follow instructions. Future books in the series include pilgrimage, fasting, prayer, and retreats.